CAR KUNG FU

A Complete System of Economic Self-Defence for Canadian Motorists

ROBERT APPEL

McGraw-Hill Ryerson
Montreal Toronto

For Mr. and Mrs. Willy

First published in 1991 by
McGraw-Hill Ryerson Limited
300 Water Street
Whitby, Ontario, Canada
L1N 9B6

1 2 3 4 5 6 7 8 9 10 AP 0 9 8 7 6 5 4 3 2 1

Canadian Cataloguing in Publication Data

Appel, Robert, date
    Car kung fu: a complete system of economic
self-defence for the modern motorist

Includes index.
ISBN 0-07-551054-5

1. Automobiles – Handbooks, manuals, etc.
2. Automobiles – Maintenance and repair.
3. Automobiles – Purchasing. I. Title.

TL151.A77 1991   629.28'722   C91-093141-0

Book design: *Michelle Losier*
Cover illustration: *Stuart Knox*
Inside illustrations: *Stuart Knox*

Printed and bound in Canada

Contents

1

The Car Kung Fu Philosophy

Which of the following motorists will best benefit from the Car Kung Fu philosophy?

1. Jane Doe is a single parent with limited financial resources. She suspects that used cars are a better buy than new ones but simply doesn't want to take a chance on unexpected repairs. She is determined to buy new, and she will happily fork out the money for the "extra-cost" warranty — unless someone convinces her differently.

2. Budd Rudd is almost at retirement age and wants to drive a vehicle that is not only stylish but also a financially smart buy. Budd wants a car that is likely to appreciate over time, whether new or used.

3. Smart Bart is on a budget. A serious budget. He has only $2,000 to spend and he wants the most car for his money.

4. Patty knows that something is not quite right with her 1985 Asteroid. But she is not sure what to do about it.

Should she go to the dealer? And what about that
friendly fellow who runs the corner garage — can he
handle it? On the other hand, there is that chain across
the street with the "guarantee that is good across the
country." Or should she listen to her brother Fred who
keeps telling her, "Just drive the car. Don't fix it if it's
not broke."

5.   Worried Walter is in a pickle. He knows his '86
Whizzbang is worth only about $3,000 from his in-
surer if he crashes it, but he simply loves the car. And
the body shop on the corner wants $1,500 to make the
car "like new." If Walter puts the $1,500 in, will he
ever see it again? And what if the car is in a serious
accident? What then?

Answer: *Each* of these people can benefit from Car Kung
Fu. Read on!

If this book were a car, this would the precise moment for
you to get behind the wheel, touch the controls, move the seat
around, and generally determine if you are going to be comfortable on the forthcoming ride.

Basically, this is the time for us to let our hair down and
get to know each other just a bit.

Me, I'm known as a car expert.

Actually, I hate the term "expert". In my day-to-day ef-
forts, I am continually learning new things about cars, and
also having to relearn the things I thought I already knew.
Still, in this hustle-bustle world of ours, people like to classify things up-front. And I guess I classify as "expert."

In the sixties, when I was still in university, I taught a
weekend course in essential car maintenance and operation.
That course, which has evolved and changed quite a bit over
the decades, is the substance of the book you are reading: *Car
Kung Fu.*

In the sixties, cars were different. A *lot* different. By
buying a standard $20 kit (containing a neon timing light,

dwell/tach, remote starter, and spark plug wrench) it was possible to tune up 99% of the cars on the road in the privacy of your own backyard. With the odds of success in your favour, at that.

Today, you could buy $100,000 worth of equipment and still be extremely limited in the range of cars you could fully tune. And that assumes it is still possible to tune a car — which it isn't. (More about that later!)

NO MORE MR. NICE PERSON

When I ask you to think of Car Kung Fu as you would a martial art, I'm not kidding. And, as in the case of a martial art, to make the most of the skills you will be learning you have to be prepared to use them without mercy on your opponent. In boxing language, you have to "take off the gloves." Of course, I am not saying that every encounter with a provider of an automotive good or service is a call to action. Far from it. However, your skills must be kept sharp and ready. You never know when they will be needed.

In 1977 I was in the process of writing an automotive handbook for a small publishing company. It had never done a car book before but had been successful with a diet book and a book on baby care, so it reasoned a car book wouldn't be too far afield.

After my first chapters were submitted I received a very concerned call from the editor. "You make some very strong statements about some of these companies," she pointed out. "There must be a way to tone this down...?"

At first I thought that the publisher's legal people had made an objection, but further into the conversation I realized that this was not the case. I had simply encountered, for the first time, the "statistically correct" car consumer, the kind of consumer whose continued existence in the marketplace allows the auto industry to do what it does to us with impunity. The kind of person who truly believes that everyone out there in Carland "means well," that it is in bad form to say or think unkind things about a car maker, and that, if nasty things need to be said, someone in the government will do it for us.

In the course of book, I hope, dear reader, to impress upon you that the car game is really not a very nice game to play.

Or pay. That the system is weighted against you, Jane Q. Public, to a degree that makes Las Vegas look safe. That the least damage you can expect as a typical automotive consumer is to get about 50 cents' worth of value for every dollar you spend. And, in an extreme case, you may end up spending a huge chunk of your income for a vehicle that will never transport you or your family around reliably or safely.

I will remind you, over and over, that the car business is a zoo. And, when the feeding cart comes by, you're what's on it. With a few exceptions, this billion-dollar industry is almost totally unregulated for plain old-fashioned quality. Safety, maybe. Emissions, sure. Value — who knows? An unimaginable percentage of the so-called "car news" you read in magazines and periodicals is simply recycled pap. Much of it originates with the very car companies being "reported on" in the stories. (And, since the publications need the companies' advertising, they simply republish the propaganda they get "as is.") In like manner, the bulk of the car reviews you read in the major magazines — the ones you'd think were beyond reproach — emanate from reviewers that rely on the on-going good wishes of the car companies to get a continuous, free supply of product for their testing. (Some publications, like *Consumer Reports*, are a rare and welcome exception.)

In my career I have been fortunate to "break" a car story every now and then — to come up with a story that no one else had done before. I was, for example, the first journalist in North America in the seventies to do a national story on the benefits of rust-proofing with oil-spray. And, following that, I was for many years a lone voice in the wilderness when I pointed out to a mystified public that tune-ups don't really exist anymore. Yet as late as 1989, while doing a story for a major home renovation magazine, I got a call from the editor of the publication that reminded me so much of that earlier experience I have told you about. "In your story you say that tune-ups are obsolete," she said with obvious irritation in her voice. "You must be mistaken. My garage did one for me just last week!"

Plus ça change....

In the sixties, most of the vehicles on North American streets were domestic. And in those days "domestic" was to be taken literally — all the parts of the car were made here. Today "domestic" might even include a Honda — a Japanese design made and assembled in North America!

Also, during that era, the car manufacturers had cleverly managed to convince us that putting a different skin over the same mechanical parts made for a different car. *Ergo,* a Chevelle was different from a Cutlass was different from a Skylark was different from a Lemans. In fact, all the cars produced by the major domestic manufacturers were remarkably similar mechanically. And, as a result, they shared hundreds of common parts.

One more thing: in those days, the use of electronics under the hood — aside from essentials like batteries, ignition parts, lights, and fuses — was almost unknown. Most moving parts of the automobile did just that: they moved! And, as such, they were able to be repaired by the simple process of disassembly and rebuilding.

CHOP! KICK! PUNCH! #$

Here is Car Kung Fu in action. A former student went to a muffler shop because she noticed that her muffler seemed loud. On the hoist, it was obvious the muffler and tail pipe needed replacement. As she watched, the technician approached the underside of her car with a large mallet and swung back to "test" the remaining portions of the car. "Stop that!" she screamed in her best Car Kung Fu voice. "But I have to check the rest of the system," the fellow protested. "Check it with your eyes, or your hands, not with a hammer. How would you like it if your doctor used a hammer on you every time you went in for check-up?" The car owner successfully limited her repair bill to muffler and tail pipe only — not bad since most muffler shops prefer selling a complete overhaul. She knew the rest of the system was old, but if it lasted one more season it was still money in her pocket — wasn't it?

Another story, one of my favourites, concerns a fellow living in Montreal, who purchased a popular — and expensive — Japanese sports car at a dealership. Within days it was apparent that something was not right with the vehicle. When driving at highway speeds, with the steering wheel pointed straight ahead, the car had an alarming tendency to pull to the right. The buyer went to the dealer's mechanics but received no satisfaction. He complained to the service zone manager for the Montreal area. When he finally got his meeting, the manager looked him straight in the eye and said that the car pulled to right because the roads in Quebec slanted to the right. End of story? Not quite. Here our Car Kung Fu graduate did an amazing thing. He contacted Transport Canada, the Canadian government watchdog for highway safety, and asked for the correct forms to report a "safety" problem. (He realized, of course, that the mere thought of a safety investigation keeps car makers up at night. A recall could cost them millions of dollars). Before actually completing the paperwork, he contacted the manufacturer's head office in Toronto and explained in glorious and graphic detail exactly what he was up to. Within 24 hours, a three-person team of Japan-trained mechanics flew into Montreal to work on his car. Two days after that, the car's suspension was fixed — more likely rebuilt — to his satisfaction.

Putting all these factors together — a handful of manufacturers, many models sharing a core group of parts and components, and the very real option of being able to repair worn parts instead of having to replace them — you end up with a very different picture of the car business from the one we have today.

None of these changes has anything to do with inflation. As far as I am concerned, you can leave inflation as a constant and *assume* that car prices are supposed to rise along with the price of bread and coffee simply as part of the natural order of things. (In fact, car prices over the last 50 years have always outpaced the base inflation rate — but let's not get picky at this stage of the lesson.)

What I am talking about here are the *repair and maintenance* options that used to be open to the average car owner. Because there were, relatively speaking, so few parts scattered over a such a wide selection of models, the typical car owner then had something which today's motorist cannot even conceive of.

Choice.

If you needed a particular part for your car you could, of course, go to the dealer. Doing so (then, as now) guaranteed you a brand new part at the highest possible retail price in the prevailing marketplace.

Or you could go to your local parts store and shop the "aftermarket." The "aftermarket" was a generic term for all those secondary manufacturers who went into business making replacement parts that, generally, were as good as or better than the manufacturer's — but at a much lower cost.

The reason the businesspeople who supplied the aftermarket could do this was that, overall, there were not that many parts they had to make. And each part was pretty simple, straightforward, and relatively inexpensive. This is no longer true today.

There are now a lot more models and makes on the road and, for reasons that are still not clear, very few share common parts. The parts themselves are no longer purely mechanical but more in the nature of electro-mechanical. That is, they have electronics meshed in with their mechanical bits.

Nor are today's parts simple. For example, many of the computer sensors and modules sold for today's cars are so sensitive that even incorrect handling could destroy them. This has resulted in a policy at the wholesale level which prevents the garage from returning the part unless it is proven to be defective. This means that if you, or your service technician, order the wrong part in error, or buy a new part merely to "swap-check" the old one and later find the old part is still OK, then you cannot return the new part. And these errors are expensive — most computer sensors retail for between $200 and $1,200.

CAR PARTS: THE OLD VS. THE NEW

Shocks   An outlay of $30 each and $10 for installation used to do it. Now, on most cars, the shock/strut assembly runs about $150 per wheel, and then tack on another $75 or so for installation.

Headlights and Tail-lights   Many of today's new cars have sexy designs that integrate the headlight or tail-light lens assemblies right into the car body. Looks great — until you get a bump or stone chip and have to consider replacing the thing. Prices for headlight/tail-light lens assemblies start at about $100 and can run as high as $600. And don't forget there are — count 'em — four to a car.

Alternators and Starters   As recently as a decade ago, a rebuilt starter or alternator could be had for considerably less than $100. Now most of the newer units, especially on Japanese cars, are both downsized and lightweight. They are also difficult, if not impossible, to rebuild. Or take apart. Or repair. So, if you want one, think new. Think original manufacturer. Think expensive. Think pain. (Prices vary between $200 and $650.)

Mechanical Fuel Pumps   Not so long ago, a $30 part at the local parts shop. Now most are 100% electronic, sometimes carrying more chips and transistors than your friendly home stereo. There is also very little standardization from make to make or even model to model. Figure $200-$550, and hope the replacement unit lasts longer than the first one did.

Digital Gauges   Used to be that when a gauge on the dash bit the biscuit, you either fixed it or replaced it. And replacement used to be well under $50. Now, thanks to modern technology, you don't replace just one gauge, you replace the whole dashboard. (The individual gauges on digital dashes are totally nonserviceable.) Cost varies between $250 and $2,500, depending on make, model and the position of the planets.

Wheel Bearings   Prior to the popularity of front-wheel drive, these bearings were considered "expensive" at $20. Now figure about $150 per wheel, plus labour.

Car Brains   Most cars on the road today have at least one ECM ("electronic control module") and about a dozen or so sensors that feed the thing information. These units, smart as they are, don't understand the meaning of the word "fix." Or, for that matter, the word "cheap." When they act up, you don't repair them, you replace them. The cost of the ECM itself varies between $400 and $2,500. The more complicated sensors (such as the ones that monitor air flow) can easily run $350-$650, plus diagnostic time, plus installation. Plus aspirin.

OK, Car Kung Fu students, what's the bottom line? It's simply this: because of the complexity and variety of the parts needed for today's cars, the "aftermarket" has shied away from making a lot of the parts they used to make. At the aftermarket level you can still pick and choose among simple things (spark plugs, mufflers, brakes) but, once you get into the more complex fuel or ignition components, you're on your own. Or, more precisely, you're "on" the dealer! Because no one else can supply the precise part you need for your car. And if you think the dealers have responded to this situation by keeping prices low, then I have some swampland in Missouri I'd love to show you. Most dealers have, in fact, responded by computerizing their inventory, much as the supermarkets have done. So if you need a part that the dealer himself purchased a year ago, the price you will be quoted for the part will be the price set by the computer the same day you come in to buy it — usually much higher than the retail price when the part was originally stocked!

But lack of choice when it comes to securing parts for your trusty vehicle is merely the tip of the iceberg.

The ability to make major or minor repairs is now also far beyond the ken of the average car owner.

To put it another way, the DIY ("do it yourselfer") has been forced into early retirement.

On today's modern automobiles, there isn't really that much left to do. Even if you are bored and really want to do something.

The advent of electronic ignition, silicone wires, platinum spark plugs, and computerized fuel injection means, practically, that the tune-up, the so-called "minor servicing," has gone the way of the dodo bird. (This doesn't mean, however, that no one will *sell* you a tune-up.)

Pop open the hood on any modern vehicle. Notice that the amount of working room around the engine area has diminished to the point of farce. On the cars of yester-year, you could — possibly — stand inside the engine compartment, between the engine and the fender, while you worked. Today, the ability to see even a speck of roadway when peering into the engine compartment probably means the designer didn't do his job right. He obviously didn't make use of every available centimetre of space. (It is indeed lucky that spark plugs last as long as they do, because on many of today's cars the plugs are changed "blind," by touch and feel only, and the operation often requires the removal some other component — such as the air conditioner — to get access!).

HOW CRAZY IS THIS INDUSTRY?

A few years back *Car and Driver* magazine did a moderately unkind review of a new Buick offering. To appreciate fully what happened next you have to keep three things in mind. First, the review was not obviously negative — that's a no-no — but, rather, it was not obviously positive. Second, *C&D* was then, as now, the biggest car magazine in the game, a real media force. And, third, then, as now, *C&D,* like every other car magazine, big or small, relied for its cars on the ongoing largesse of the company being reviewed — in this case, GM. In the issue following the review under scrutiny, *C&D* reported on a very unusual subject: themselves. Specifically, they explained that the day the Buick review hit the stands, GM phoned to say that, due to an administrative error, the Buick on loan had to be returned. Immediately. Within hours, a GM car jockey showed up to collect the keys. Such incidents, by the way, are not atypical — and credit should be given to *C&D* for pointing out to its readers what was happening behind the scenes.

There are many other examples. A Canadian car industry analyst was a guest speaker on a podium which included the then-president of GM Canada. The analyst made some remarks about GM which, while not insulting, were not exceptionally positive either. (This was at a time when GM's performance was not particularly positive.) That afternoon the fellow received a call from a secretary at GM cancelling their subscription to the analyst's newsletter. With such behavioural examples to follow, is it any wonder that buyers of lemons sometimes feel compelled to set their cars afire on the manufacturer's lawn as a means of getting attention?

And the opportunity for DIYs to do damage — to both themselves and to their pocketbooks — is higher than ever. Electronic ignitions produce enough current to stop your heart should you ever touch the wrong part of the wire accidentally. And the parts themselves have changed also. Most of the electronic components under the hood are extremely sensitive to the installation technique used. Forget to add a dab of grease here, or to tighten a connection there, and the part could readily fail two weeks after the repair. ("Fail" here means destroy itself, and necessitate a new part.) Even stranger, the routine servicing of certain components may actually require "retraining" the master computer that controls your car's most essential operations. In the late eighties, for example, certain Ford products had central computers that would "forget" their initial settings if the battery power was cut off for more than 20 minutes — as might happen if the battery had to be changed or serviced. Resetting the computer was no easy feat: it required a lot of training and some very expensive test equipment. Chryslers from the same period used similar technology in their transmissions. Cut battery power for a few minutes and the next time the vehicle started it would seem surprisingly "rough" in the drive-train for the first few days. Mechanics would later discover, to their absolute horror, what the real problem was: during the power shutdown, the transmission's built-in computer would have forgotten the correct "shift points" that were stored in its memory and, for several days after the power was cut, the system would behave like a small child learning how to walk. Or, in this case, when to shift for itself!

AS EASY AS IT LOOKS?

I have a vivid — and frightening — memory of walking by a young man who was busily turning a wrench under the hood of his Japanese import. As is my nature, I could not help stopping and watching. "Whatcha' doing," I asked. "I'm changing this part," he said, indicating a box on the ground near his foot. "Saving a fortune. Friend of mine showed me how." "Fine," I replied. "But what are you doing right now?" "Oh this?" he said. "I am getting this tube out of the way so I can install my part." "Do you know what that tube is for?" I asked him. "I think it has to do with the brakes," he said. "Yes," I responded, "that's a brake fluid line. If you open that line up you will almost certainly get air into the system. If you get air in the system, you will have to bleed the brakes...or you will end up having no brakes. To bleed the brakes, you will need a hoist, some special tools, and you'll have to know what you're doing besides. If you don't have an idea what I am talking about, I think you should stop what you're doing right now...don't you?" He did.

Let me put this yet another way: if you open up any older car book you are likely to notice that some 50% or more of the material is about all the neat things you can do to your car at home, in the privacy of your own backyard. *Rebuild your carburetor! Check that timing! Set those points!* What'ssamatter? Your dashboard clock doesn't work? *Pull that dash out! Let's fix that clock!* Fuel pump on the fritz? *Grab that wrench! Yank that pump!*

Today this attitude simply won't fly. Fuel pumps, to take one example, have been moved on many cars from the engine compartment to the inside of the gas tank. Servicing them requires first draining and dropping the tank — not something most of us would want to do while waiting for Sunday football to come on the air.

Today it can fairly be said that the degree of complexity of the modern auto is such that working on your own car is a worrisome, not to say expensive — and possibly danger-ous — pastime.

But — here's the kicker — does all this necessarily mean that you should throw in the towel, reach passively for that wallet every time your car needs work, and resign yourself to overpaying for your car's needs for the rest of your days?

I hope not!

Because avoiding this fate is the absolute essence of Car Kung Fu. I teach an essentially philosophical and informa-tional approach to car purchase, ownership and maintenance. A major study done by the US government once established that up to 50 cents of every dollar spent on your automobile is wasted or spent needlessly. The very word "waste" implies that there is a more efficient way to get the same results but with less money. Making the right choices, having the correct data to work with — this is the key to car ownership in the nineties.

Not having the right wrench set; having the right information.

Car Kung Fu, the book, is based on Car Kung Fu, the course, a course I have been giving on and off since those first college days of mine in the sixties. A course in strategy. A course in making choices.

A course in saving money.

If you think about it for moment, you'll see that making the right choices is as much a part of car ownership as punching the pedal and hammering the brake.

If you are thinking of buying a car, for instance, the choices facing you might be:

- Make and model?
- New or used?
- Lease or outright purchase?
- Foreign or domestic?
- Options?
- Extra cost warranty?

Then, as time goes on, you will make choices like:

- Minimum or maximum maintenance program?
- What sort of shops to patronize?
- What kind of insurance to get?
- How to keep the car's appearance up?
- How to combat rust?

And, as you get to know your car over the years:

- What does that noise mean?
- The car is old — it is worth it to have it fixed?
- What is this car worth anyway?
- Am I taking safety risks?

- What maintenance schedule should I follow?
- Is there anything I can do myself?

Well, you've come to the right place. Car Kung Fu is pure strategy. It can help you handle these decisions, and make the right choices. I remember once a student of mine wrote to tell me about his experience getting an alternator changed at a large chain store:

As you suggested, I stuck an electrician's meter into the cigarette lighter outlet first to check the output of the alternator. It was clearly below normal and, since the car was over five years old, I decided a replacement was a good idea. The dealer price was around $300, but the local chain store price was about $75 below that, and their guarantee was quite well known. So I gave them the work. I knew I had already saved myself about $30 by doing the diagnostic part, and I remembered clearly what you had said about "doubling up" on common jobs. The alternator belt was due for a replacement and, since they would have to take it off anyway to change the alternator, I told them to change the belt at the same time. When I came back to pick up the car, I found two separate labour charges: one for replacement of the alternator, and one for replacement of the belt. I could see the problem: the shop computer had been pre-programmed with labour charges for each, but no one had anticipated the customer's voluntarily asking for both jobs at once. I pointed out to the service manager that the alternator replacement included the belt removal so, in effect, I was being double-charged. Now here is the wacky part: the service manager had trouble following this and had to confer with a mechanic before giving me the proper credit. This absolutely confirmed what you had said about most service managers' having no technical training; that, if they really were mechanics, they could make more money in the back working on cars! Thanks again for the advice. Because of your course, I saved not only money but aggravation as well!

BANANAS IN THE CRANKCASE!

Sometimes you teach things that you don't intend to. In my course I make a point about the various additives that are sold to retard oil burning. The bulk of these are just expensive "thickening" agents that increase the VI (viscosity index) of the oil. They work for a few months only, postponing the inevitable. I tell my students that, before these things were invented, owners used to put bananas or sawdust in the crankcase. Months after one course, I heard through the grapevine about a student who had a full-sized Chevy V-8 with one cylinder showing zero compression and a lot of valve noise. He had become something of a legend in town because at every oil change he would show up at the garage with a banana and ask the attendant to put it in with the new oil. (That, plus the fact that the car tied up bay space while the oil took 30 minutes to drain, had turned the fellow, and his vehicle, into local celebrities!) If anyone asked, he would give *me* the credit for the idea. According to what I heard, he did drive that car an additional 60,000 km before the poor thing finally bit the biscuit! (Note, dear reader, that, in spite of this peculiar tale, such a method is not particularly recommended. An engine less hearty than a Chevy V-8 would likely have self-destructed in short order. And, since I was able to test drive the vehicle in question during the "fruit fix," I can testify from personal experience that engine performance was considerably less than satisfactory.)

Like the martial art after which it is named, Car Kung Fu gives you, the reader, leverage. It allows you to deal in the most expeditious manner with a direct frontal assault on your pocketbook.

It contains the best of all the tips and tricks I have gleaned in my 20-year career. A career, by the way, which has included a visit to *Good Morning America,* regular guest spots on a half-dozen major TV shows in Canada and the US, three car books, a weekly radio column with a PBS affiliate in the US, the longest-running syndicated radio show in Canada's broadcast history, and hundreds upon hundreds of test drives of vehicles of differing makes, models and nationalities.

And yuppy beware! This book may not be for you! The advice contained in Car Kung Fu is clearly and unequivocally at odds with that character the comedian Billy Crystal used to play on *Saturday Night Live*, the one who used to say, "It's not how you feel that's important ... it's how you look." In Car Kung Fu it's not how you look ... it's what it costs you to get there.

In the next chapter we will look more closely at the positioning of cars in the marketplace and we will see clearly that many people today drive cars not so much to reach their destination, as simply to be seen to be reaching their destination. I am talking about those people who don't "drive" cars, they "wear" them.

YOU ARE WHAT YOU DRIVE

Researchers in West Germany recently completed a study which showed that drivers with red or yellow cars tend to be more aggressive and less courteous than drivers of cars painted in quieter shades: blue, for example. Can it be that our choice of car reflects in some way our personality? Let me know whether or not you agree with my own observations.

I have noticed, for example, that drivers of BMWs are more likely than other drivers to cut you off or change lanes quickly. Similarly, if you get off to a slow start at a stop light, the most likely tail-gater you're going to see in your rear-view mirror is a BMW. It's almost as though, having paid so much for a car which is supposed to be fast, these drivers have to continually prove that they meet the standards of their car.

I have also noticed that Hyundai drivers simply want to be left alone. If anyone were to invent a paint that causes invisibility, I think the first buyer would be a Hyundai owner.

And speaking of vehicles that say things about you, did you ever notice that Jaguar owners will park their vehicles just about anywhere? I'm not kidding — sometimes I think that, if the urge overtook one, a Jaguar owner would vacate the car right in the middle of a major highway, motor running.

And last but not least, what do you think of anyone that is still tooting around these days in an old VW Bug? There are not a lot on the road anymore because, in case you haven't noticed, they stopped making these things decades ago, and parts and service are no longer very easy to come by. This means that anyone still in a Bug is likely putting quite some effort into keeping the thing running. For what reason? Status? Snob appeal? Or maybe there is some kinky thrill in driving a car that looks like an insect, sounds like a blender, and forces your nose up against the windshield during tight turns? Perhaps, deep down, that's the real motivation behind buying any car. Most of us aren't simply trying to get somewhere. We're also trying to find ourselves.

Of course, this is nothing new. The original "you are what you drive" credo was fostered by the likes of Cadillac and Lincoln over half a century ago. The makers saw clearly, even then, that people would be prepared to spend more — sometimes even a lot more — to be perceived as being better off than, or superior to, their neighbours.

Whether or not you were, in fact, getting anything for your money was quite another story entirely:

- In the beginning, cars like Lincoln were hand made, and the premium paid was for true extra costs during the manufacturing. By the end of the century, however, virtually all luxury cars — especially domestics — were completely mass-produced. The premiums were still there, only now they represented profit. Pure profit.

- In the seventies, Ford went so far as to take one of its base models, gussy it up, and sell it as a Lincoln (the Versailles). GM, for reasons that will never be clear, liked the same idea enough to bring it to Cadillac. First they whipped up the Cadillac Seville by grafting odd parts onto a Chevy Nova chassis. Then, years later, the same company tried to sell an overdressed Chevy Cavalier as a Cadillac Cimmeron. After the first bout of bad press, however, Cadillac changed the name to "Cimmeron by Cadillac," leaving the marketing people a little room (two words' worth actually) to separate themselves from the car if things got any worse.

- *Consumer Reports* once pointed out that a Chevy with all the options was a better buy — and possibly a better car — than a base Cadillac.

- Although in Germany Mercedes models are so common that they are used as taxicabs, the company had the foresight, when coming to America, to market its products as top of the line only — and charge a hefty premium for them. The strategy worked. You don't see many Mercedes taxicabs over here, do you?

- In the late seventies, BMW, like other companies, got caught by the US emission laws and were unable to deliver a car that kept the performance standards previous models had met. (One example was the BMW 320.) By this time, however, the BMW had become so well positioned as a "yuppiemobile" that it took members of the public almost three years to realize they were being sold less car for more money. (Eventually the 320 was dropped from the BMW North American line completely.)

To sum up: Car Kung Fu is not for people who *wear* their cars to work. Car Kung Fu is for people who *drive* their cars to work.

Car Kung Fu is for people who are bound and determined to get the most kilometres for the least cash. People who sincerely want to get a dollar's worth of value for every dollar they spend on their vehicle.

Over the years I have driven everything from the cheapest third-world imports to the most prestigious luxury cars. From Hyundai to Porsche, from Renault to Mercedes. In spite of the wide differences in pricing among these cars, the truth is that they all had common characteristics by which they could be judged. Looks. Performance. Gas consumption. Comfort. Handling. Relative cost and complexity of parts and service. Most important, they were all cars. They were all designed by the maker to get you there, and get you back.

Car Kung Fu says, in a nutshell, that leather interiors are nice. CD players are also nice. Sunroofs are a lot of fun if you like to look at the undersides of bridges.

But the bottom line is where you're going, and how much it's going to cost you to get there.

It's that simple.

2

Know Your Enemy: An Unabridged History Of The Motorcar

QUOTE WITHOUT COMMENT

In 1990 *USA Today* polled a random sampling of new-car dealers to see which marque they thought to be the best. The winner was Honda, a brand actually vended only by a relatively tiny proportion of the dealers surveyed....

When was the very first motorcar invented? It should surprise no one to learn that even this seemingly simple fact is a hotbed of contention in the car industry. The problem has to do with the theory of synchronicity: that different people in different places, each ignorant of the other, could come up with the same thought, the same concept, the same invention. It would seem that while the motorcar was being born in North America, it was simultaneously being midwifed in

Europe. Renault and Daimler Benz, in particular, may be among the oldest pedigrees in the car game.

An equally interesting question might be, "When did it become obvious that the motorcar was more than a mere labour-saving device; i.e., that it was itself a symbol, an icon, a tactile representation of ideals and lifestyle?"

The answer to that second question is equally obscure. We know that early in its development the motorcar was little more than an expensive toy, a bauble for the idle — and sometimes not-so-idle — rich. We know that only with the economies of mass production in the 1920s did the cost of the car drop sufficiently to make it possible for "average" men and women to get their hands on one.

A LOT OF CATCHING UP TO DO

Jeff runs a rust-proofing shop that guarantees its work. Every now and then a customer will come in with a problem and, if the customer has played by the rules, Jeff will absorb the cost of the repair. Still, over the years, Jeff has learned a important lesson: "First I check if it's a domestic or a Japanese product," says Jeff. "Often the rusting or bubbling is simultaneously covered under two different warranties: my own and the original manufacturer's. The one offered by the manufacturer expires first, of course, but sometimes there is that overlap. If so, I will recommend that the customer ask the dealer for satisfaction first, because the dealer will have the equipment on the premises to make the body repair quickly and expertly. What I have found over the years is that, if the car is a Japanese product and the original new car warranty hasn't expired, the dealer will make the repair. If the car is a domestic, however, the dealer will stall and stall and stall. Try to wear the customer down, I guess. So I will just take it on the chin and pay for the repair on my end. Still, over the years I've wondered how many customers the domestics have lost with that kind of attitude. It's scary."

We also know that the marketing of the automobile is a phenomenon, an economic force, quite separate and apart from the product itself — a trend that began over half a century ago and has continued unabated until today.

Since Car Kung Fu is presented as an economic martial art, practised in a skills arena where theory and comprehension are everything, we will take a moment here to pursue some of these thoughts in more detail. "Know Your Enemy" is our buzz-line. Many consumers operate under the facile delusion that the car industry operates just like any other business, like a dry cleaner or a corner grocer. In fact, that is not true at all.

The car industry is one of the closest examples you are likely to find of what the economists like to call an "oligopoly" or "near monopoly."

When you buy something that is available to a degree which more or less matches its demand, you will probably end up paying a price which is more or less "fair." On the other hand, when you buy something that is in limited supply but has moderate to high demand, you will almost inevitably end up over-paying or, at least, paying more out than you are getting in return.

THE UNEXPURGATED HISTORY OF THE GLOVEBOX

When was the last time you put your gloves in the glovebox? No kidding. Many parts of the modern motorcar have names which, believe it or not, are buried in antiquity. Many of these names make reference to functions or factors that simply have no relevance today. The glovebox is one example. At one time, in the automotive equivalent of prehistory, people put their gloves in there. Now we use them to store owner's manuals, maps, glasses, chain store coupons, gasoline receipts, cameras, parking tickets and even the occasional cheeseburger. But gloves? Not very often.

When was the last time you put a trunk in your trunk? Yes, that's right — in days gone by, when a car was still called a horseless carriage, trunks and other baggage were fastened to the rear end of the vehicle. That's where the name "trunk" comes from.

And if you think "glovebox" and "trunk" are the only oddities, think again. There are lots of car part names that don't quite mean what they say. Bumpers, for example. When was the last time you used your bumper actually to bump anything? In fact, for most of this century these things were so fragile and delicate that the slightest tap or bruise would bend them completely out of shape and lead to a good-sized repair bill. Now they're built a bit sturdier. Now, theoretically, you *could* bump into something with one. If you really wanted to, that is. When was the last time you used your emergency brake in a real emergency? Most people use them to park on hills occasionally and that's about it! Speaking of emergencies, when was the last time you used your emergency flashers in a dire situation? Double-parking in front of the dry cleaner doesn't really qualify, although it seems to me that's the only time I ever see these things in service. Here's a doozie: What does your fan belt do? If you think it spins the fan, you're wrong. Almost all cars now have electric fans. The fan belt on most of today's cars spins either the air conditioner or the alternator. Do you fasten your seat belt when you get behind the wheel? No, you don't: you use something called a lap and shoulder harness. Simple front seat belts disappeared way back in the sixties. How much brighter are your high beams compared with your low beams? Time's up! They are exactly the same brightness. The bulbs merely point in a slightly different direction! And, finally, is antifreeze really there to keep your car from freezing in cold weather? The right answer is yes — and no. Modern cars use a pressurized water system that is actually more likely to boil over than it is to freeze. Modern antifreeze keeps the engine from freezing up — and boiling over too!

Let's not mince words: the car industry causes you to pay out more than you get in return. It always has done this and it always will. Of course there are laws against what I'm talking about, but no country in the world has ever had much success enforcing those laws. Ironically, the greater portion of the used-car market operates in exactly the opposite way. All over the world, it is the marketplace alone that determines what a chassis and set of used wheels are really worth — one more reason why a used car is an interesting alternative to buying new, in the Car Kung Fu philosophy .

And the process is made all the more insidious by the fact that in the car business you don't even need outright collusion to keep prices high. All you need is "a gentleman's agreement" of sorts — a collective unwritten understanding that when you raise your prices, everyone else will raise theirs too. (This process is described in some detail by former auto magnate John de Lorean in his book *On a Clear Day You Can See General Motors*.) And now, let's determine what is being done with all this extra money consumers are paying — or, should I say, over-paying. It would be nice if one could assume that over-payment in any industry had definite long-term benefits for a society; that, for example, over-paying an auto worker resulted in a happier auto worker, or over-paying for a vehicle resulted in a slightly higher quality vehicle. In fact, as will be shown below, neither of these conclusions holds up under scrutiny.

When you dig down beneath the glitter, the chrome, you are left with an essentially gluttonous industry that repeatedly charges one a lot for a little, relative to other commodities. An industry where it is assumed that you will over-pay not only on purchase but all through the use and maintenance cycle of your vehicle as well. An industry where excess is the norm, not the exception. An industry so accustomed to outlandish margins that it can, in bad times, afford to drop thousands of dollars off its list prices, issue juicy rebates directly to buyers, and offer financing at rates that would make a banker salivate — and still make a profit! You are left, in a nutshell, with the car business.

Where did the madness start? The post-World War II era was a strange time for the car industry. In North America production had been cut back during wartime and, as a result, pent-up demand was beyond everyone's expectations. Everyone wanted wheels. This was the only time in the history of the motorcar when dealers were heard to complain that they were being bilked by customers! Here is what was happening. Demand for used cars rose with demand for new, and dealers were buying everything that drove, or was wheeled, onto their premises, often without much opportunity for a full inspection. So the dealer would trust the word of the seller that the car was "in good shape," or "had a good engine," or whatever. One older dealer told me that during this period he bought a trade which "ran a bit rough" at highway speeds. When he put the car on a hoist, he found a rotten two-by-four tied in where the metal drive axle should have been!

Coincidentally, this was also the era when the horsepower race began in earnest. Given the low cost of fuel (actually, like most commodities, it can be perceived as low only with hindsight!), the manufacturers did not hesitate for a second to see who could come up with the larger engine, the shortest 0-60 time, the best quarter-mile lap. This disquieting trend would continue unabated until the late seventies.

During the same approximate time the cars themselves were changing, although the changes, ironically, were often less than they seemed. If one browsed through the literature of the fifties and sixties, one would come away with the impression that every year the makers had brought out some incredible piece of technology which was going to change, once and for all, the way the world worked. Turbo-hydramatic transmissions, rocket engines, ram-air intake manifolds — these were the buzz-words that promised tomorrow's technology today.

In fact, what the customer usually ended up with was yesterday's technology tomorrow. Again with the benefit of hindsight, we can see now that the North American industry during the two decades after World War II had completely deluded itself into thinking that it was master of its own destiny, that it knew precisely what was happening.

History repeated itself — at the consumer's expense. Years earlier, GM had trounced Ford by demonstrating that buyers would actually pay a premium for a car that looked better but didn't actually perform any better. The industry had learned from the experience and learned well. In the Detroit of the post-war era the designer was king. At the manufacturing plants events were clearly prioritized. First, the "look" of the car was completed. Only then did the engineers get a chance to find out what components, if any, would fit under the hood. The public didn't really begin to notice what was happening until, on a few ill-fated models, mechanics would complain that the only way to change the spark plugs was to remove the engine first!

CAR KUNG FU IN ACTION

I want you to meet a student of mine named Gary. Gary had a British convertible sports car which he loved. The zipper on the convertible cover broke and no one, but no one, wanted to do the repair. In desperation, Gary called several places in the southern US that catered to collectors such as himself, and was finally quoted a range of $90-$150, plus shipping. Then a light went on in Gary's head. If the problem was only a zipper, why not call a zipper company? Gary found a zipper company in his own city that had the right zipper in stock. One problem: they refused to deal with Gary, a humble member of the public, directly. Gary waited five minutes and phoned them back. "Gary's Auto Repair," he said, "Gary speaking. Can you sell me a zipper?" A day later Gary had the part he wanted. Cost was 80 cents. Installation? By now Gary was getting pretty darned creative. He took the convertible cover and the zipper to a shoe repair. The total bill

came to $12, a savings of approximately 90% on the quotes
he was getting from the so-called specialists. The moral of
the story is that there are many ways to skin a cat, many
ways to fix your zipper, and many ways to fix your car!

The big "three and a half" (GM, Ford, Chrysler and sad
little AMC) were like whales wallowing on the beach, paus-
ing occasionally to flick sand in each others' faces with a
twitch of a flipper. They produced similar cars, similarly
priced, and — no surprise — similarly engineered. They
charged about the same for their cars, so consumers didn't
have a lot of bargaining room regardless of where they
shopped. If it were possible to pinpoint three over-arching
strategies that dominated the industry during this period, they
would most assuredly be:

- Make it bigger.
- Make it faster.
- Make it more expensive.

The simplicity of these goals belies their earnestness. Each
maker was unabashedly shameless in pursuit of size for its
own sake. And the extremes to which each was prepared to
go to achieve this end would make even Machiavelli blush.
GM and Ford, in particular, saw nothing amiss in bringing
out cars clearly positioned in the compact to mid-sized market and then, during subsequent model years, increasing the
length and wheelbase of these models until the so-called
economy-sized car resembled a small condominium.

As for horsepower, one simply could never get enough. It
was at this point in history that an entire generation of young
people with serious buying power appeared on the market.
(Today we know these middle-aged connoisseurs as
yuppies.) They did not find anything contradictory in com-
mandeering a 1,300-kilogram vehicle with a 375-horsepower
engine to get them to work and back. Not to mention having
the occasional race — among friends, of course — to see

whose car could break warp speed in the best time. (Recently, a major car magazine tested a '68 Buick GS 400 in an attempt to emulate the road times for which the car had been noted when it first appeared. Try as they might, the editors could not get numbers that matched the performance recorded in the original archives. A long-time reader wrote in with this helpful tip: "You have to pile shaved ice on top of the intake manifold to get the performance up. That's what we used to do.")

And, finally, as far as pricing was concerned, Detroit saw itself limited only by its own fevered imagination. Until the late sixties, the makers had at least showed the grace to withhold price increases to one per model year. However, once that psychological barrier was cracked (and it cracked readily), then up to a half-dozen price increases per model year failed even to raise an eyebrow. Nor did anyone stop to ask why, when the cost of *everything else* in known civilization was staying fairly constant, the cost of cars was rising like bread on a hot day.

Bigger. Faster. More expensive. These were, need I emphasize, ominous signs. Some experts have speculated, with reason, that had these trends been left to develop unchecked then, by the eighties, we might have ended up with Detroit products that would not fit in any indoor garage, would outperform a medium-sized prop plane, and would use so much gas that, if you left the engine running while you pumped the gas, you would never fill the tank up. A horrible thought to contemplate.

Fortunately, however, destiny came early to the car industry. In the late sixties a series of events began that brought to Detroit a combination body-slam, pile-driver and sleeper-hold, the likes of which it had never seen before. The first of these was government legislation of emissions.

By the late sixties the governments in the US and Canada were bold enough to demand, with the force of legislation to back them up, that the cars stop spewing out garbage while their engines were turning over. The car makers had been quite spoiled by the fact that, generally, the government had left them pretty well alone for decades. The one exception had been in the matter of automotive safety, which had become regulated, to some slight degree, in the early sixties. Some say even *that* might never have come about if GM had not put a private eye — a shamus — on the trail of a then-obscure lawyer named Ralph Nader, to discredit him and make him stop saying nasty things about the Corvair. The new legislation was a shock to the makers. For Big Brother to show up one day and demand that cars run cleaner was, for Detroit, the equivalent of telling them what to make, or even what to charge. And it was a basic, rock-hard tenet of the auto industry (then, as now) that nobody ever tells Detroit what to charge. Ever.

The hearings and lobbying which were the inevitable run-off of any such complex piece of legislation started off badly. Essentially, no matter what the government asked of Detroit, the experts would simply say it could not be done. This itself had several additional repercussions. Although some form of emission control technology had begun to appear on all cars, by law, as early as 1968, it wasn't until the late seventies, a decade later, when "serious" regulations began to be passed. "Serious" because, if one listened to Detroit, there was no known technology available to meet the standards that the government was so busy mandating. An extraordinary bit of theatre was taking place in Washington (and, by proxy, in Ottawa). The government would ask for the "desirable," the car makers would respond with, "Impossible," and the legislators would proceed "unstoppable."

Meanwhile, technical types the world over watched this drama unfold and wondered just how Detroit would meet the new standards. Detroit's most fearsome lobbyists were turned loose with the message that the politicians had, in essence, gone mad and the emission goals were impossible to meet by any method known to modern science. With hindsight, we know that this was one case where the bluff and bluster of the motor companies had some basis in fact. The government actually did pass progressively more stringent emission laws that were to take effect in the future, without any clue as to how the auto companies were going to do what they were supposed to. Luckily for all parties — the government, the car companies, and us — computer technology came on the scene in the late seventies and made a lot of these "impossible" demands possible.

While all this was happening, the Detroit marketing people scurried in to report the shocking (but fairly obvious) conclusion that the biggest engines were also the biggest polluters. To put it another way, the biggest profit makers were also the biggest liabilities in terms of the new clean air laws.

Detroit was given precious little time to solve this dilemma before the other shoe dropped: CAFE, or corporate average fuel economy. In the seventies Americans were given a quick taste of their own medicine. They found what it was like to be buyers of a commodity that was in short supply and for which the sellers could charge whatever they pleased. Specifically, oil. They were given a taste of what it was like to stand in line and beg for gasoline — and it was a taste that they found most disagreeable.

The result was yet another series of new laws. This time they dictated to the car companies how much gasoline their cars could use. This new legislation gave the companies an average fuel efficiency number that their entire fleet had to reach each year. And, in opposite manner to the earlier legislation calling for declining emissions, these MPG numbers actually *increased* from model year to model year.

So now those same marketing mavens who had brought us the "horsepower wars" were back in the board rooms complaining that the engines that made their buyers happiest — the giant V-8s — were also the engines that polluted the most *and* gave the worst fuel efficiency. Ouch!

It would have been nice for the manufacturers if they had had a fallback plan of some sort. It could have been either of two strategies: a whole new series of really neat *small cars* that didn't need such large engines; or, failing that, a whole new series of high-performance *small engines* that could nimbly move around the large amounts of sheet metal their customers had grown so used to.

In fact they had neither. As history would later attest, Detroit was then (and, by its own admission, was until recently) completely incapable of doing a really good job of building a stylish, functional, smaller vehicle. And, as for the problem of building a better but smaller engine — well, that's still another cup of worms. With lots of hindsight, we now know that Detroit *could have* reached into its magic hat and pulled out some decent hardware. But to do so at the time would have taken a damn-the-expenses, full-speed-ahead attitude that Detroiters have never really shown. Instead of seeing the problem for what it was — deadly serious — Detroit chose to patch everything up by just reaching out and grabbing the engines it already had — pathetic little four- and six-cylinder jobbies held over from the forties — and plopping those down inside its long, wide and heavy sheetmetal.

It was really a neat trick, and, in other circumstances, it might have worked. If not for two little words: foreign competition.

THAT OLD FAMILIAR DASHBOARD

Recently, when I was picking up a Mercedes 300 SE for testing, I asked the company representative if there were any special instructions before I started it up and drove off. Special controls, new instruments, that sort of thing. "No," said the quite pleasant lady as she handed me the keys to a $75,000 motorcar. "They're all pretty much the same."

Hours later, the comment she'd made was still ringing in my ears. *They are all pretty much the same.* If you've ever driven a Mercedes, even once, even if it was decades ago, then you know you can hop into any model currently in production and feel pretty darn comfortable behind the wheel. The configuration of all Mercedes automobiles is still front-engine, rear-drive. The instrumentation is still all gauges; you won't find any digital junk nesting inside a Mercedes. The climate is still controlled by a strange little wheel that is covered in brightly coloured numbers. All you have to do is turn the wheel until you get just the temperature you want. A child could manage it. And the ignition switch is still on the dash near the lighter, right where it always was. Back in the sixties, when the governments of Canada and the US mandated locking steering columns, almost all the car makers in the world moved the ignition switch to the steering column because it was convenient for them. But not Mercedes. The steering column does stay locked until the key is turned, just like the government says. But the switch itself is right where it always was, on the dashboard.

The more I thought about it, the more I realized that this car company actually goes *out of the way* to make things seem comfortable and familiar. Virtually all the cars that come from Detroit and Japan these days have buttons and switches that change from model to model, even year to year. But a Mercedes is a Mercedes is a Mercedes. It's almost as though the car company was sending a special message to its customers: If you care enough to buy our cars, we care enough to make sure that the controls are easy to use. It's a short, simple message. And coming from one of the most successful car companies in the history of the industry, it may well be a message the competition should heed.

This is perhaps old ground. Books have been written about the way Detroit "ostriched" itself as the foreign manufacturers set out for American shores. And, at first, it really was all quite innocent. The British, French and Italians had product to sell, but they weren't seen as a real threat: c'mon, really, the quality isn't there, parts and service are strange, and everyone knows that foreign cars are small and tiny, not really *American*.

But — and it would take Detroit almost a generation to re-alize this — small cars did not have to be unpleasant. Prop-erly designed and built, they could do all the things a car is supposed to do: provide a sense of fulfilment to owners, and, best of all, meet all those ornery emission and fuel economy laws in the process!

Unquestionably, this alone was a lot to contend with. But hidden inside this invasion force were two foreign players that we haven't yet accounted for. Welcome, please, the Germans ... and the Japanese. And this was where the tide really turned for the domestic industry.

Of the German presence in North America's auto markets it can at least be said that Detroit was given a lot of warning that something was happening. Nothing too specific, mind you, but signals were being sent. While the VW Bug was never, by any stretch of the imagination, a "fine motorcar" (I should know — I owned a couple!), the spiffy marketing of the product on US shores, and the high degree of owner satisfaction, should have told Detroit that its act needed work. While never a truly great car, it was good car that, amazingly, got better from model year to model year (something I challenge anyone to say of the Detroit products of the era). And, while the Bug had no great pretensions, it did deliver faithfully the things it originally promised to. The fact that it was actually watertight — a phenomenon di-rectly resulting from the close machine tolerances to which the body was built — made it part of American culture, in a series of jokes of the era.

Meanwhile, at the other end of the price spectrum, the gutsy marketing strategy of Mercedes (and, to a lesser extent, BMW and Audi) was beginning to pay off. While Cadillacs were changing size from year to year like the mythical Gulliver, with the German imports you knew where you stood. You were paying a lot, sure, but let's not under-emphasize this: you knew what you were getting. I have always felt that Mercedes, more than Holiday Inn, deserved the slogan "No surprises."

ONE ZILLION GUINEA PIGS

One of the great metaphysical questions if all time is, "What kind of car quality would we have had from Detroit if all these things (the events discussed in this chapter) had never happened?"

We will never know for sure, but the signs were ominous to say the least. Through the seventies, the publication *Consumer Reports* noticed an increase in the average number of defects per domestic car looked at. About the same time, the domestic makers cut back severely on their warranty programs after determining that their cost of actually servicing the warranties, at no charge, was too high. (In the eighties, squared off against the imports, they had to go back once again to better warranties.) Consumer spokesperson Phil Edmonston, in the seventies, went so far as to advise never buying any car model in its first year because all the technology was essentially unproven.

For my money, the biggest tip-off as to where we might have been headed was the GM X-Car line launched in the late seventies as the company's answer to the problems of fuel shortages and imports. The X-Car was an unmitigated disaster. The car was not only a poor, badly designed machine but, if the lawsuits that mushroomed around it can be taken as an indication, a dangerous and possibly lethal vehicle as well. Had it come from any other car company in the world, the X-car would have been dismissed as good intentions with bad execution. But, in fact, it sprang from the loins of the largest car company in America, a company that had had the better part of a century to get its act together. As in the case of the Corvair and the Vega before it, GM proved once again that, as a domestic market leader, it had no shame when it came to selling a product that wasn't quite ready for the real world. One might include in the same breath the infamous Cadillac 4-6-8 engine of the period, the multi-talented engine that could do anything you wanted it to — except run your car; also the infamous Olds V-8 diesel, a powerplant that GM had cobbled together from a gasoline engine, and that, in real service, demonstrated the approximate durability and toughness of chiffon.

With these examples in mind, anyone wondering in what direction the American industry was headed need perhaps look no further — and wonder no more.

You might think that Detroit would have noticed these trends, and viewed them as ominous. It didn't. And, with yet another case of night-blindness, it stood amiably by while the most serious invader, the Japanese, hit American shores.

Whether or not those first Toyotas and Datsuns (a.k.a. Nissans) were miracles or messes remains to this day a controversy. Consumer advocate Phil Edmonston, former head of the quasi-militant Automobile Protection Association, dismisses virtually all the early Japanese product as "headgasket-a-day" junk. On the other hand, I had hands-on experience with several of the earliest Japanese products to reach these shores and, in my experience, the worst-built Japanese car of that era met or exceeded the standards of any domestic product of the same time.

But let's not mince words. Japanese cars had several things going for them:

- low prices;
- astounding quality;
- fantastic gas consumption;
- an efficient — and responsive — marketing apparatus;
- "damn the torpedoes" technology.

Price and quality we need not dally about. Suffice it to say that the defect levels that Detroit considered normal in the early seventies were anathema to the Japanese. Zero defects was and, as far as I know, still is their goal.

As for gas consumption, the Japanese had a bit of an advantage. As net importers of oil, they were no strangers to high gas prices, and all their vehicles had to have good fuel efficiency in order to sell in their own domestic markets.

Those last two points deserve a word or two of explanation. Whenever they were faced with a technical challenge, the Japanese exhibited a trait that the domestic makers shied away from: they quickly scrapped older designs and started with a clean slate. This greatly worked to their advantage as the combined emission control and CAFE regulations came into play in the North American market. While the domestic makers recycled 20-year-old technology into their Chevys and Monarchs, the Japanese approached the problem from scratch. The result, for the foreign makers, were cars with smaller, cleaner and more economical engines than anything Detroit could have conceived. Some have said that the Japanese were subsidized in this by their own government. Be this as it may, Detroit was hardly a "hard times" industry by the time the seventies rolled in. It had just come out of one of the biggest car booms of the century. It had the cash to spend on new technology — all it lacked was the guts.

All this could be taken to mean that the import manufacturers were to become some kind of salvation for the hapless overcharged consumer; that the import invasion was the economic equivalent of the cavalry showing up on the doorstep.

Not true.

Two things happened next. Detroit ignored the Japanese — sort of hoping that they would disappear if left alone. And, whether because of or in spite of Detroit's attitude, the North American consumer fell in love with Japanese products. Not like. *Love.* I'm talking head-over-heels, stars-in-the-eyes passion. There is no other explanation because, by the early eighties, it became clear that consumers would actually pay a *premium* for a Japanese product, compared with the going rate for an equivalent domestic product.

At this point in our story — we are now well into the late eighties — things started to get really sticky. By this time the domestic makers, having had the better part of two decades to resolve the problem, had decided, "If you can't beat 'em, join 'em." Ford and Mazda were, if not outright married, at least engaged; GM was seriously dating Isuzu and flirting outrageously with Toyota; and Chrysler — one of the first of the domestics to meld with the Japanese — was deep in a love-hate relationship with Mitsubishi. (Love because the foreign product sold well in Chrysler dealerships; hate because, if supply had been infinite — which it wasn't — the Japanese models would have outsold the domestic models, yielding a lower profit for Chrysler.)

The ultimate exponent of these two decades of irony could be found in a series of TV commercials done in the late eighties. These ads featured Lee Iacocca. In them, the automotive potentate complained bitterly about consumers' prejudice against domestic products, pointing out that in Chrysler dealerships where identical imported cars were sold — one bearing the Japanese name and one with an ersatz domestic badge — the foreign nameplate outsold the fake domestic. And that held true even if the domestic-badged product was set at a lower price!

If this was prejudice, it was prejudice deserved. Considering Detroit's witch-hunt against Nader; its refusal to acknowledge first the European and then the Japanese car invasions; its stubborn refusal to scrap engine designs which had already yielded about three decades of profits (and depreciation); its inability, now or then, to make a decent small car; its willingness to use its oligopolistic position to raise prices for no other reason than to raise prices; its casual attitude to vehicle quality accompanied by a willingness to use the consumer as guinea pig wherever possible; and many more like crimes against consumers too numerous to list here, it can safely be said that the mavens who ran Detroit got more or less what they deserved.

THE CASE AGAINST GM

If you are closet GM-basher, or just curious, you might have a peek at the book *Dead Reckoning* by Maryanne Keller. Keller is an auto industry analyst of some repute. In this work she describes the saga of General Motors during the 1980s. And a sad saga it is.

During this period "the General" lost huge chunks of market share, a great deal of profit and considerable public respect. It was during this era that GM spent hundreds of millions of dollars on hi-tech robotics only to watch its cost per car rise — while its competitors, using uninspired old fashioned "people" technology, *reduced* their costs and made greater profits. It was during this time that GM paid out, again, hundreds of millions of dollars for the EDS corporation, an acquisition which it figured would solidify and ensure its future in hi-tech.

Along with that particular purchase came an unexpected extra: Ross Perot, EDS's outspoken and mercurial founder. After the acquisition, Perot, who was partially paid in GM shares, went poking about trying to see how GM *really* ran, and how his new investment was really doing. And, in the process, he ticked off so many people that GM paid out tens of millions of dollars just to buy him off and send him away.

It would be easy, when dealing with a company of this size, to blame everyone equally, but Keller doesn't take the easy way. *Dead Reckoning* quite explicitly lays the blame for all GM's ills with one lone character: its cold, calculating, and quite impersonal chairman of the day, Roger Smith. Although the fallout from Smith's reign may not be fully appreciated until the late nineties (Keller's book, released in 1988, is carefully ambiguous on the subject), it is clear that the workings of the company clearly reflected the workings of the man. It is indeed ironic that, by the very end of Smith's reign, the only GM division showing signs of health was Cadillac, where a near mutiny by management had resulted in a return to larger, heavier body-on-frame vehicles — exactly the kind of cars Smith had ordered into oblivion.

But what did the consumer end up with? Well, by the late eighties there was good news and there was bad news. The good news was that the domestics had, by this time, had their noses rubbed in their sins more often than an errant puppy. Selection was never greater — the best products from companies all over the world were now found in dealerships. Also, quality had never been higher: the very presence of the Japanese in the marketplace had improved the gene pool. Every other maker had not only to improve internal quality but also to prove to the consumer that its products really were better. The first domestic to do this was the Buick division of GM. When the division found, to its astonishment, that it was producing some of the most trouble-free cars in the world, it didn't waste a second taking full-page ads to tell the world about it. Good stuff. About two decades too late, but good stuff.

And now the bad news. The pot-pourri of events that had changed the car game — and almost levelled GM — left behind a strange and terrible legacy. Cars were no longer cars. It was that simple. Price aside, the mechanical beastie that sat in your driveway in the early nineties bore little resemblance to its counterpart of the sixties. The type of steel that made up its shell was different. Its wind-cheating design was different. The light space-age materials that composed the interior were different. Underhood there were chips and sensors doing things that purely mechanical parts used to worry about. Even the tires were different — using different rubbers, different rims, and sporting new computerized tread designs! And with all these differences came a shocking realization: service was no longer as easy, or as available, as it used to be. Unless you were prepared to trade as soon as the warranty expired (and, statistically, few of us really are) then the very process of finding and purchasing service for your vehicle was going to be very different from the way it had been.

And there was more. The Japanese, in their conquest of domestic car share, had picked up a few bad habits from their enemies. They had come to appreciate the power that comes from being able to charge more for a vehicle merely because demand is greater than supply. By the end of the eighties the prices of Japanese cars had begun to skyrocket. Worse, it was the Japanese — and not the domestics — who perfected the "wear it, don't drive it" marketing stratagem that GM had first toyed with in the thirties and forties. Honda, easily the most outrageous and aggressive (and perhaps most shrewd) of the Japanese firms, decided to out-Cadillac Cadillac and out-Lincoln Lincoln. In spite of reviews that said that their best-selling Accord model was already one of the most perfect automotive machines of all time, they set out to resolve the question of whether customers would fork out over double the price of an Accord for a slightly larger and slightly more comfortable car. The answer — a resounding "yes" — fostered the Accura Legend and began years of infighting among Japanese makers for the "more-money-than-brains" yuppie buyer.

And, dear reader, the car game has never been the same since.

HISTORY IS NOT OVER...UNTIL IT'S OVER

The reader may note a certain predisposition in this chapter. Detroit — especially GM — comes across looking less than pristine, and the Japanese industry practically sparkles with valour and goodliness. Is this the way the world really is? Maybe. In 1990, when this book was researched, that was the way things looked. Detroit had bungled the ball so badly that four generations' worth of successes were reversed in less than one. And Japan was beating literally everyone at their own game: manufacturing cars in America better than the natives ever did and taking over the high-end luxury market — once the exclusive preserve of the German industry — car by car and customer by customer.

Whether or not these trends will hold for the next decade, only time will tell. Robert Stempel at the head of GM is no Roger Smith — luckily for GM. His moves seem bold and bright. His attention to product, not numbers, is deserving of respect. He has the will, the way and one of the largest economic powers in the world to work with. Let's hope he does something with all that power. And as for the Japanese — they have consistently shown only two genuinely virtuous traits during their short conquest of the industry: a passion for quality that borders on obsession, and a reaction time to consumer needs that would make a professional athlete envious. Both these qualities have been lacking in Detroit for decades. On the other hand, the Japanese have shown a number of disturbing qualities also. Among these are:

- A willingness to abandon the low-end of the market because there is not enough profit in it. Without this market they never would have been able to get into North America in the first place.

- A "bigger-longer-wider" fascination every bit as outrageous as Detroit's. *Car And Driver* Magazine noted that, over a decade, the Honda Accord grew from a spiffy and roomy little compact that delivered over 45 m.p.g. to a quite presentable mid-sized model that delivered less than 25 m.p.g.

- A penchant for charging whatever the market will bear that would make even Detroit blush.

- A complete lack of interest in what might happen to older models of its cars. (In truth, the only company of note that has ever realized the importance of trying to make its older fleet look respectable is Mercedes. My sources tell me that the company has tried to keep the price of body panels for its older models low to encourage owners to make repairs. Mercedes understands perfectly that new car sales benefit when older models stand out.)

- Espousal of technology for its own sake. Like Detroit, the Japanese are too quick to use new technology simply because it is new. The newer Japanese models use things like electronic suspension and transmission, which deliver only marginal benefits yet promise huge repair costs down the road.

3

Buying New, Without Getting Blue

There is an old car biz joke which goes, "'How do you make a car salesman feel as though he's died and gone to heaven?' Go over and say, 'I must have that car. Price is no object!' Then let nature take its course....'"

Buying new?

Before going any further, I must ask you, beg you, implore you to stop and make sure you really want to do this. I make no attempt to hide the fact that my personal preference is for a used vehicle (see the next chapter). While it is quite possible to use Car Kung Fu to get good value on a new car, the odds suggest you will never come out as far ahead as with a used, or even slightly used, machine.

Now let's look at the new car game and see how to play it to win.

First, make no assumptions. A lot of people assume that the salesperson genuinely wants to help you, the buyer, arrive at a deal that is fair for both sides. Poonswaggle. As Tony

Randall once pointed out to Jack Klugman in a classic *Odd Couple* episode, when you "assume," you make an "ass" out of "u" and "me"! Although the moral righteousness of car salespeople has never been the subject of a major Yankelovitch survey, there are reliable indicators to the effect that it is not really very high. In other words, if the salespeople could sell you a $10,000 car for $15,000 plus your first born, they would. They are simply trained to be that way.

And boy are they trained! Today's modern automotive salespeople are as much a marvel of technology as the products they vend. They are likely attending seminars during their spare time to learn new and better techniques for closing sales. Such ripe plums as "Never ask a question that can be answered negatively" and "Always act as though the buyer has *already* said yes" are programmed into their impressionable young minds week after week.

And then there is *you*. You buy a car only every five years; the last major purchase *you* made was sushi a la carte; *you* are completely overdrawn on your VISA card; and somehow, still, you have conjured up the certainty of the blessed that *you* are going to win this particular encounter. Possibly that conversation you had at 3:00 a.m. last night with Uncle Joe has more than equipped you for the tough negotiating job ahead. The adrenaline is pumping. Brain cells are firing like little spark plugs. The Force is with you. You are prepared.

Prior to arriving at the dealer's, you have scrupulously read at least three major car-oriented consumer magazines. You have deliberately left your cheque-book at home so you will not be bluffed into offering a down payment on a car before you are ready to buy. You have watched three *Dirty Harry* re-runs and mimed all the dialogue in the mirror. You even called Sly Stallone's house, collect; told him to get a speech coach; then hung up. You're tough. You're strong.

And, the moment you walk onto the showroom floor, you're dogmeat.

Face facts. If the car industry weren't so able to extract the last thin dime from buyers such as yourself, there probably wouldn't *be* a car industry in the first place. Think about it.

TIME TO TRADE

When:

1. Small children gather outside your house at 7:00 a.m. to watch you try to start up.
2. The mechanics say they don't carry parts for an import — and you're actually driving a domestic.
3. You overhear your youngest daughter explaining to a neighbour that your religion forbids you from entering a new car dealership.
4. You are using up an awful lot of gas — especially when parking overnight.
5. You search the dashboard for something digital and all you can find is the serial number.
6. Your in-laws *agree* that your car accurately represents your own unique personality.
7. Your insurance company asks that the car be safety-certified and, after you have it done, insists on a second opinion.
8. You stop for gas in small town, and the attendant said that, if you don't turn the engine off, he will never be able to fill it.
9. You notice that the starter motor on your engine is larger than some of the newer Hondas.
10. Your dog crawls under the seat — and is never seen again.
11. Your favourite downtown parking lot won't accept your business anymore: the attendant says two cars can fit comfortably where yours normally goes.
12. Your tires are wearing, but not on the tread.
13. Your wheelbase is too wide for those pull-through car washes.

14. Police routinely pull you over to check for guns.
15. In a moment of weakness, you have offered to *give* the car to your 16-year-old nephew, the one out on parole. He turns you down.
16. You go to a body shop to get an estimate on new paint and they *assume* you have come for collision work.

On the other hand, use my extremely powerful Car Kung Fu techniques and you may just have a chance.

Here are a few pointers:

1. Make up your mind beforehand.

Decide on all the important stuff *before* you start seriously dealing with the salesperson. Decide on make, model, options, colour, trim — even on the extras and add-ons. Every time the well-trained salesperson asks you one of those "helpful" questions (the ones designed to make you feel you have *already* purchased the car) tell him, or her, to take a hike. Remind him that all you want to talk about is *price*. And if the price isn't right, you're gone.

2. Do your homework.

One of the best deals around is the little-known service offered by Consumers Union (the same people who publish *Consumer Reports*). For a small fee, they'll run a computer search on the make and model you want, and reveal to you the base US retail and wholesale prices for the car and the options. The more you know about what the car costs the dealer, the better position you are in to deal. (See Chapter 11 for more information.) In Canada (where retail prices for most things are dictated by complex tax tables and possibly the position of the planets) you can make use of this data to calculate the true mark-up the dealer makes on the wholesale price. Then, working with the Canadian retail, work backward to guesstimate the wholesale.

3. Declare your intentions up-front.

Salespeople are exposed to so many flaky customers they sometimes think they work for Kelloggs. In a pleasant way, explain that you are in the last stages of the buying process. It is not "if" or "what" that is the issue, but rather "how much."

4. Don't fall into the trade-in shell game.

Going in to close a car deal with a trade-in that is unpriced is like having a "sure thing" in a horse race but being unable to find your wallet. By the time you get things sorted out, you may well have missed your chance.

PARTS PRICING

A recent story appearing in a major magazine showed that the front bumper on a Mazda minivan cost $329 while the same part on the Chrysler minivan cost only $75. Similarly, the tail-light lens for the Mazda cost $17 while the same part for a Nissan minivan cost $45 — and so on. But do you know what the magazine forgot? They forgot to *add up* the total of the dozen or so parts that were included in their survey. To have done so would have disclosed which cars cost the most to service. So I did it for them.

My conclusions (based on a minivan review that appeared in *Popular Science*) were that, of the four brands tested — Chrysler, Nissan, Mazda and Ford, the parts for the Chrysler were the least expensive. We've all heard rumours about how costly foreign cars are to fix, but, from this report, I calculated that the Ford actually cost more to repair than the Nissan. The highest parts-basket cost went to Mazda, which is not surprising. As any Mazda owner will attest, Mazdas don't need repairs often but when they do, it hurts. I can recall once shopping for the flasher unit on a Mazda GLC — that's the part that lets all four lights blink at once in an emergency. On most domestic cars that's a $20 part. On a Mazda that's a $90 part.

The point of all this is not just that you should bring along a pencil and calculator every time you read a car report. The point is that the cost of service and parts for some cars can be dramatically different from the cost for other cars. And, with information of this type available, its best to have the facts at your fingertips before you buy.

Car dealerships are not exactly non-profit operations. If you really want them to take Old Nellie off your hands, without fuss or bother, they will. But you'll pay dearly for the privilege. The usual mark-up on a trade-in is *at least* $1,500-$2,000, and stories of $450 trades being resold *the very next day* for $3,200 are not uncommon. Ask yourself, therefore, whether running a private ad (and putting up with those strange phone calls at all hours) is worth that extra cash in your pocket!

And, as I suggested above, beware also of those dealers who try to confuse the trade price (the net cash allowance on your old car) with the so-called discount on the new one. Frisky salespeople have been known to quote excessively generous trade-in allowances, only to grab back the gift later on when it comes to discounting the new vehicle.

Never bring that trade along with you when trying to close a deal. If you are not selling your trade privately, then bring it to the dealer where you intend to buy your new car at a time of day when your friendly new car salesperson is *not* on duty. Ask specifically for the Used Car Manager, say that you've just taken a job out of the country, and that you want a fast, fair cash price for the car. When the manager makes you an offer, make a note of the amount. *That's* what your trade is worth, no more and no less.

Often, when the buyer tries to trade and buy *in the same transaction,* the salesperson will accidentally lose the buyer's keys for an unspecified period of time. This makes the buyer a captive audience while the deal goes down. However, by following Car Kung Fu techniques you can avoid this problem completely.

PLAIN OR EXTRA CHEESE? (MAKING CHOICES)

Domestic or foreign? Feeling guilty about shopping the imports? Well, here's a peculiar but accurate rule of thumb: you can buy foreign cars at a domestic dealership but, generally, you cannot buy domestic models at a foreign dealership. GM, Ford and Chrysler all seem to have forsaken the notion of ever producing a decent small-sized sedan under their own steam. To compensate, they have each resorted to acquiring (or joint-venturing with) overseas companies that have already mastered that task. To highlight just of few of these mixed marriages, GM blithely sells cars made by Suzuki and Toyota, Chrysler unabashedly vends Mitsubishi products, and certain Ford models share chassis and mechanical parts with Mazda to a degree that is possibly embarrassing to both companies. Simply put, you can't tell the players without a score card. All in all, your best bet is still simply to choose the car that appeals to *you,* on a purely hormonal level, and leave the politics to the politicians.

CASH FOR THAT CRASH!

A 1989 study on crash repair was conducted by the US Insurance Institute for Highway Safety. The Institute, as you may have gathered from its name, is absolutely *obsessed* with car crashes and the costs associated with fixing up those crashes. Every year it buys several million dollars' worth of new cars for testing. Then it proceeds to simulate crashes of those shiny new models by smacking them into fixed objects at a controlled 5 m.p.h. crash speed. The cars are repaired and the cost of the repairs carefully scrutinized. In theory, if all the manufacturers were doing their best to build safe cars *and* keep the cost of replacement parts in line, then the repair costs would be about the same for all cars. But, as the Institute found out, theory doesn't count for much in the car game. *The average repair costs among the cars it tested varied significantly.* The *lowest* repair bill resulting from this standard crash simulation went to the Ford Escort which required only US$382 to make it whole again. The *highest* repair cost from that same test went to none other than Honda. Fixing the body parts damaged on a new Honda CRX model required a whopping US$3,140 to get everything back together. Wow! Another groaner: Cars that did poorly in the test were the Korean built Pontiac Lemans and the VW Jetta — both of which required about US$2,000 to fix the damage. Almost *all* the Toyota models tested, on the other hand, did incredibly well, requiring, on average, only about US$750 to get back on the road again.

Keep in mind, however, that no matter what you buy, your *true* cost of ownership will include not only fuel, lubrication and maintenance, but also — that hidden scourge of driverdom — depreciation.

Depreciation can be as high as 40% in the first year. One day the car is worth $10,000 and the next, so it seems, the car is worth only $6,000. My how time flies! To minimize depreciation, you should seriously consider selecting either an especially "hot" design which is likely to hold its own over the coming years (as, for example, the blisteringly successful Mazda Miata, not so much a car as a recapturing of errant youth) or, failing that, a marque which has proven itself over time to depreciate considerably less than the norm. In the latter category, these brands specific deserve very special attention: Mercedes, BMW, Volvo, Jaguar, Honda and Toyota.

Is buying a model in its first year a good idea? Well, consider the seemingly similar sagas of two recent sportscar entries, that infamous Mazda Miata and its domestic precursor, the Pontiac Fiero. Putting a down payment on the Miata when it was first introduced would by now have qualified you for MENSA. Being the first into the garage for the Fiero, during its introduction, would merely have earned you a large headache and a sore pocketbook.

Overall, brand new models do tend to be more trouble-some than their tried-'n-true siblings. But all it takes is one Miata every now and then to remind you that rules are made to be broken. If there is a lesson to be learned, it's simply this: be careful out there! (If the car companies really need you to test out their products in the real world, fine: let *them* pay *you* for it. And not vice versa.)

Options? Well, you don't need a Ph.D. to understand the new car brochures. But it helps. Take for example, the interesting distinction between front drive, rear drive and 4-wheel drive. Front drive means that the engine is located in the front and powers the two front wheels. Rear drive leaves the engine in the same place but powers the two rear wheels. Four-wheel drive, meanwhile, has become a catch-all term that could mean any one of three distinct configura-tions: a front-drive car which has the ability to power the rear wheels occasionally, as needed; a rear-drive car that has the ability to power the front wheels, as needed; or a vehicle that has *all* four wheels under power at *all* times. (If you find this confusing, imagine how poor car salespeople must feel — their livelihood depends on getting this straight!)

In choosing, consider the following insights: Front drive provides better traction in the snow than rear drive. You pay the price, however, in higher maintenance costs during the later, more mature years of the car's life. Four-wheel drive technology of any kind virtually *guarantees* you will never get stuck anywhere for as long as you own the vehicle. The trade off, however, is much poorer fuel economy throughout the vehicle's life, and much higher than normal maintenance costs as the vehicle ages.

Other popular techno-treats offered on today's new mod-els include things like turbo-charging and supercharging, both of which should be scrupulously avoided unless you have an uncle in the repair business who happens to owe you money. Last, but not least, are the so-called option and trim packages. (You will almost never come across such marketing shenanigans at a foreign car dealership, yet, for reasons that elude me, our domestic marketing mavens can't seem to function without them.) As a rule of thumb, assuming your budget permits, you should OK anything that makes the car look better, run better or last longer. Keep a sharp eye out for items marked with "HD" or "heavy duty." Such options almost always accompany worthwhile mechanical enhancements that make the car more durable over time (HD radiator, HD suspension, HD battery, etc.).

The two most glaring exceptions to the rule about grabbing the appearance options are *any* waxing package or *any* rustproofing package. Research suggests that car dealers are incapable of offering either of these seemingly worthwhile services at fair rates, and, if you allow either or both to be foisted upon you, the slick salesperson may well end up with a larger commission for *this* than for the *car*!

Lease or buy? Watch out. Although there is, generally, only one way to truly "'buy," there are now as many variations of leases as there are flavours at Baskin Robbins. If you are even thinking of leasing, make sure you take nothing for granted about the deal you're being offered. Have each clause explained. And then explained again. When all is said and done, however, there is still only one person who is optimally qualified to help you decide whether or not to lease: your own personal, trusted accountant. Leasing, for all its glamour, can cost you up to 40% *more* than an outright purchase. Its main advantages are an improved cash flow resulting from a lower down payment, lower ongoing payments during the lease and, more often than not, significant tax breaks when the vehicle is used for business purposes. Whether or not this trade off works in your favour is a decision for the C.A., and *not* the friendly car salesperson.

TO LEASE OR NOT TO LEASE?

According to experts, there are now almost as many different types of leases as there are cars. One government study found 12 critical areas of the contract in which small variations *now* could cost you big dollars later on. When the leasing salesperson hands you the nicely printed form to sign, he or she will no doubt give the impression that the document in question has been carved on stone tablets by some higher power. Fuddle duddle. The fact is that the lease was most likely written up by the lawyer for that particular company and it is likely quite different from the leases drawn by the lawyers for all the other leasing companies.

For example, some leases include maintenance in the cost of the lease, and some don't. Some leases allow you almost unlimited kilometres, and some don't. And some leases specify that you can loan the car to other friends or business associates, and some don't. More importantly, some leases specify that you have the option of buying the car at the end of the lease yourself for a fixed price, and some don't. This can be important because, if the car in question has held its value, you may want to consider buying it yourself and then reselling at a profit. On the other hand, if the car has not kept its value, you want the lease to specify that the leasing company will take the car back from you with no hidden cost or penalty. Not all leases say this — you have to ask for it.

Also, dealers often make a big fuss about net payments from month to month without mentioning what the real long term costs of the car really are. It is the very nature of leasing that, after you add up all payments, interest and carrying charges, you are almost certainly paying a price for the vehicle far in excess of the maximum suggested retail price. How does that feel?

What about buying the car yourself at the end of the lease and then reselling it? Years ago, when leasing companies were relatively naive about true resale values, that was possible. Now they've smartened up. If there is hidden value in reselling the car at lease end, *they* want to be the ones to get it. The only way around this is to put a buy back option, with a set price, into the contract when you first sign it. (Also, the so-called closed lease, in which the trade-in value of the car at the end of the lease is guaranteed, may have higher overall carrying costs than the open-end type. In the open-end lease, the value of the car at lease termination is set by the marketplace, so there is an element of risk. But if the carrying costs of the open lease are lower overall than with the *closed* type of lease, it may well be a risk worth taking.)

Check all the fine print — twice. Even your warranty may depend on *your* paying the maintenance and upkeep. Neglect to maintain the car, just once, and you lose your warranty. Never assume with any lease that, if things go wrong, you can just return the car to the lessor and chuckle. I assure you, courtrooms everywhere are packed with people who thought just that way — until the trial writ was served on them.

The bottom line on leasing? In certain tax situations, it is definitely more advantageous than buying. In other situations, it isn't. Period.

And what about all those ridiculously low financing charges the car companies offer every now and then? Are they as good a deal as they seem to be? Maybe. In a clever variation on the old "don't raise the bridge, lower the river" ploy, the car companies are subsidizing lower interest rates with higher car prices. (Car prices have risen faster than the inflation rate every year since the beginning of time.) Preferred financing rates are just another cost of doing business to these companies, deserving of neither cheers nor jeers. So, if you were looking to finance anyway, you may take advantage of any special deals that are being offered. Watch out for any hidden credit or qualification fees, however; they could quickly make the bargain more trouble than it's worth!

Extra-cost warranty? Maybe. But consider this extra-cost package to be just peace of mind, really no more than an expensive one-time insurance plan that allows you to sleep better at night — for a fee. (Legally, if there are subsequent problems with the vehicle that are the direct result of the manufacturing process, you can *always* sue in Small Claims Court, regardless of what the warranty says.) There have been problems over the years with small outside insurers going bankrupt and leaving tens of thousands of owners with worthless paper instead of enforceable warranties. So, if you opt for such a plan, make sure the manufacturer's own name is behind it!

A floor car? A special order? A demo? If there is a car on the floor that has exactly the options you are looking for, by all means make an offer (see below). If, however, the floor car has options you *don't* want, resist mightily the temptation to conclude that the dealer will throw in the unwanted options just to close the sale. Cows will fly first! Your most conservative bet may be to custom order the exact car you really want, making extra sure you first *specify a delivery date on the order form*. The pre-printed form the dealers use is heavily biased in the dealer's favour and doesn't automatically fix a date. You don't have to take that: you are free to write in your own delivery date. If the dealer later misses that date, you may then get your deposit back and are free to take your business elsewhere! If you do make an offer on a demo, the price should be especially attractive, the warranty should be clear and unblemished, and the dealer should certify *in writing* that the kilometres shown are true and that the car has not been in any accidents or otherwise damaged in any way.

CLOSING THE DEAL

Books can be written on the complex mechanics of the selling and negotiating process — and they have been! Suffice it to say that, before you even start, you are outgunned, outmatched, and thoroughly outpointed. That friendly looking salesman, the one that reminds you so much of your kindly fifth-grade teacher, has sold hundreds and hundreds of vehicles to good people just like yourself who truly believed they could outlast, outwit or out-think him. *It's just not going to happen.* Time and experience have demonstrated to the salesperson that you (the buyer) dislike the haggling process so much that you will do *almost anything* to save starting over in a different dealership with somebody else. So, quite simply, the salesperson will slowly but surely wear you down. You will be actively encouraged to make an offer on the car thinking that, once you sign the offer, it's *your* car. Nothing could be further from the truth! In fact, technically, an offer is nothing until it is accepted and the salesperson's boss will not do *that* until you are repeatedly "bumped" into raising your offer to higher and higher numbers.

And here is something else you must know: in most haggling, once the buyer comes up with an offer the seller can live with, the seller simply accepts:

"OK, I'll give $200 for that vase. That's my final offer."

"Sold."

In the car business, salespeople have been playing an unusual little game for the past 100 years or so, and so far nobody seems to have caught on. The game is "It's not my job." Here's how it works.

You bargain aggressively with the salesperson for an hour or two. You fight over options, colours, tires, gauges, whatever. At some point you might even threaten to walk out unless floor mats are thrown in.

Then, finally, the salesperson caves in. "I think we have a deal," she says. "Let's write it up."

Then comes shock #1. After the deal is written up, you find that taxes, registration and special "prep" charges can add hundreds of dollars to the agreed price. (Taxes and registration you can't fight. All prep charges are fully negotiable!)

While you're recovering from shock #1, the salesperson throws shock #2 at you. "OK, sign here, and let's see if I can swing this one past my sales manager."

Past the sales manager? What this salesperson is saying is that *she had no authority to bargain with you in the first place!* Everything that has taken place so far is horse-feathers! Unless you deal with the manager, you just aren't buying a car!

But wait...there's more!

The second, but equally devastating, implication of this is that, when you sign, you aren't buying a car (i.e., accepting the dealer's offer to sell a car), but rather simply *offering to buy* a car from the dealer — and the offer is meaningless until the precise moment the dealer accepts or comes back with a counter-offer.

Yes, here's the rub, Horatio.

For economic reasons (i.e., greed) the car industry has created a scenario where the buyer, *after* hours of bargaining, makes a fresh offer to the dealership, *as if the bargaining had never taken place.*

The only similar event I can think of is the buying of a house. In that case, it is common for the buyer to make an offer to the vendor via the vendor's agent and then wait for the answer. But there are several key differences between the real estate situation and the car dealer situation:

1. When you make an offer on a house, you have not just spent an hour or two viciously bargaining with the agent.

2. When you make an offer on a house, you know, up-front, that nothing solid will happen until the vendor looks at your deal.

3. When you make an offer on a house, the offer usually says that it expires at midnight if not accepted. The forms used in car dealerships don't have expiry dates. Theoretically, you are bound to wait for their answer forever.

Now, if, in fact, "sales managers" accepted the majority of these offers as written, you would be able to say I am being paranoid, or unfair, or both.

In fact, the opposite is true. After surveying thousands of recent buyers who have taken Car Kung Fu over the years, I have confirmed that some 99% of all such offers are initially turned down by the sales manager for a variety of reasons (everything from "bad math" to "bad vibes," it seems to me).

In fact, this is exactly where the car biz really sticks it to you. The "bumping" process that takes place at this late stage in the proceedings, when you really have no stamina left, when you are regretting you ever started looking for a car in the first place, when you are dreading the prospect of having to go through all this again in yet another dealership — this is when several hundreds (or thousands) of dollars are added to the price you originally started with. *This is where the car industry makes its money!*

THREE DEADLY CAR KUNG FU COUNTER-TECHNIQUES
Sealed Bidding

This is so simple it hurts. Take a list of the car specifications you want (make, model and options) to the salesperson, smile pleasantly and explain that you used to work in the car business yourself so, logically, you are unwilling to buy a car in the traditional way.

Instead, you will allow the dealership to make you an offer on the car. (Note that the offer is *to* you, not *from* you, so you have the real power here!) Say you are taking sealed bids from five dealerships and you will open the bids next Wednesday at noon. The lowest offer to sell, in proper legal form, wins. That's all there is to it.

Reverse the Signing Procedure

This technique is not as complex but is equally deadly. When the salesperson draws up the offer to purchase for you to sign, he will quite helpfully fill in all the particulars, including the price you really want. Then he will hand the paper to you for signature. Of course, he has not the slightest intention of selling you that car at that price. Once you sign, he will begin the process I described above. Here's what you do:

1. Look him in the eye.
2. Smile.
3. Say, "I really want to buy a car from you."
4. Wait for him to nod agreement.
5. Say, "I think the price we just agreed on is a fair price."
6. Again, wait for signs of agreement.
7. Take out your watch and look at it. This should make the salesperson a bit nervous. Say, "I want you — or your manager — to sign *first*. Then I'll sign. No nonsense. And if no one signs that paper in five minutes, I'm leaving."

WHY IT PAYS TO BE TOUGH

Here is a letter from a former student that pretty well says it all:

My wife and I were looking for a van but found the prices rather high. So we decided that a one-year-old model, perhaps used or a demo, would better suit our budget. After comparing prices at several dealerships, we ran into a salesman who insisted that his price would be unbeatable. When we heard the so-called unbeatable price we didn't agree, and we told him so. We looked him straight in the eye and said that his price was outrageously high and unless he could do better we would walk out. At that point, the salesman dropped his price to a number that really did sound good, so we bought the vehicle.

> The next day we got the surprise of our lives when we showed up to pick up our purchase and we were handed the keys to the current year's model. Now here's the point: somehow during the bargaining the salesman had got onto a different wavelength from us. We thought we were still haggling over a one-year-old vehicle. He thought we were negotiating for something brand new. We were willing to walk out because we genuinely believed the price was too high for a one-year-old. For a new car, however, it was a steal, literally the lowest price in the city.
>
> The mixup got us the deal of a lifetime. But it also got me thinking about bargaining techniques. In this case my disgust with the salesman's first price was real. But clearly it is possible to get a really good deal on a new car — without any misunderstandings — simply by being a tougher negotiator!

The Appel Gambit

This technique is named after me because I was the first to reveal it in a major business magazine in the seventies. It seems even easier than the one above, but is, in fact, much more powerful. *Use it carefully! In Car Kung Fu, we never bully our opponents needlessly.*

When the salesperson presents you with the offer to sign, with the price you want, go ahead and sign it. Then, while signing, write the following specific words under your signature:

OFFER SUBJECT TO ACCEPTANCE WITHIN
24 HOURS.

Put your phone number next to your signature, smile at the salesperson, and leave. *Do not stop. Do not pass Go.*

By 9:00 the next morning the dealer will have called his lawyer only to find out that, with your conditional offer, he either sells you the car that day at that price, or loses the sale completely! He cannot "bump" you unless he gets you back into the showroom — which, of course, is not going to happen.

Two things to watch with this technique:

1. When the dealer calls to accept you offer ask for a telegram to confirm. Say you'll pay for the telegram. (It's a bargain!)

2. Don't use this technique on *another* car from *another* dealer in the same 24-hour period. You might end up with two cars!

WHICH WARRANTIES REALLY WORK?

Car companies are like the weather: you can't really guess what they will be like tomorrow by looking at how they are behaving today. Still, here is some data that may be useful.

In 1989, a major consumer magazine attempted to rate the warranty programs of all the major car companies, based on factors such as which parts are covered, rust warranty, whether or not there is a deductible, transferability, and, most important, service — that is, the ability of the car company to stand behind the warranty. They rated the companies on each of these categories, but — egad! — there was no *total* score. So I dug out my own trusty calculator and figured out for myself which company had the best overall score. The best scores for total warranty performance and coverage went to Mazda in first place, closely followed by Nissan, Toyota, Honda, Audi and Saab — in that order. At the other end of the spectrum, the worst score went to Volvo, followed by Chrysler, General Motors and Ford, in that order. What does this amazing bit of data tell us? It tells us that, in spite of their public claims of matching the Japanese at every twist and turn, the domestic makers (at the time the survey was done) were still nickel-and-dimers when it comes to warranties and warranty service. And it also tells us that, when all is said and done, the Japanese makers were boldly leading the pack in the warranty wars. And, in the car biz, you can take *that* to the bank.

THE TEST DRIVE

Say, pal: how would you like to take 'er for a spin around the block?

If you've purchased a few new cars in your day, but never heard those magic words, chances are you were born after 1950.

In the early days of the car biz, when things (and, it seems, life in general) moved at a slower pace, the test drive was one sure way to clinch a deal.

Now, nobody bothers. If you want a test drive, you will have to ask for one. And the chances of finding the exact model you want "road ready" are slim to none. You may have to compromise.

You would also be prudent to ask politely about insurance. Most dealers are covered — that's the good news. But generally their dealer policy has a high deductible, possibly in the thousands of dollars. If a question of liability should arise, and you neglected to ask in advance whether or not you are covered, then you could get hit with the bill.

This happens more often than one might think. Typically, the hapless consumer on a test will get involved in a small fender-bender with another car. If the driver of the other car gets aggressive and argues that he or she was in the right, the dealer might sacrifice the consumer to placate his insurer and get his deductible back. It doesn't happen often, but it happens. Before you test, simply say in clear English, "Am I fully covered?" If you get a "Yes" answer, that is a valid and binding legal promise.

What do you look for when you test drive? You are free to do whatever you like, of course. Play the radio. Adjust the mirrors. Open the sunroof. But here are some recommendations which, over the years, I have found useful.

Access and Egress

If you can't figure out how to get inside the vehicle, the car definitely loses points on your score-pad. Don't laugh: in the last decade many designers, bored with working on the traditional components of the chassis, began instead to tinker with non-traditional ones. The door handles, for example. Some new cars come with door handles that literally have to be coaxed out of their little cave-like recesses. In winter, snow and water make them freeze solid. Getting into your car can, in those circumstances, become considerably more of an adventure than you bargained for.

Ergonometrics

This is just a fancy word for "creature comfort." Sit in the driver's seat and, *without looking at the owner's manual,* see if you can adjust the seats, mirrors, steering wheel (optional), heater controls, radio, wipers, lights, emergency flashers and, finally, parking brake. Deduct a rating point on your mental score-pad for each control that gives you difficulty. If the transmission is manual, try to find Reverse. If the transmission is automatic, check if there are any gear ranges or appended buttons that don't make sense to you. Also, take a long hard look at the gauges. Are there any that are for measuring something you've never heard of? Deduct a point. Are there any which you were trustingly hoping to find (such as the temperature gauge) but, alas, you just can't quite locate? Deduct another point. Turn on the radio and try to change channels. Pick out your favourite channel and try to make the radio "memorize" it for later use. Can't do it? Deduct more points as necessary. (If you then can't figure out how to turn the radio *off*, deduct still more points!)

Starting the Car

Not as simple as it looks. On some cars, the starter motor will not turn over unless the clutch is first depressed. And there are stranger designs lurking about to trap the unwary. On some older Saabs, for example, you can't insert or remove the key unless the gear-shift is first placed in Reverse, which, itself, can be a stimulating mental exercise (see above).

On The Road

Here's where the rubber hits the road — no pun intended. Put down the windows, make sure the air conditioner is off and set out for an inaugural cruise along the city streets. With the air conditioner off and the windows open, you will easily pick up any loud or irritating noises in the power-train.

The first few minutes of the test drive should be spent simply getting to know your machine. What I look for is an overall integrity of design, an indication that all the components are meant to work as a team. In other words, I look for smoothness. (The smoothest car I have tested in the last few years, for example, is the Accura Legend from Honda. The car is generally so all-of-a-piece that it almost seems to know what you are going to do before you do it!)

Be careful, by the way, not to confuse smoothness with numbness. Many of the vehicles in current manufacture provide almost no feedback to the driver when turning, accelerating or braking. This "somebody-else-must-be-driving" feeling is *not* a desirable trait. Deduct points as needed.

Here's a tip: If the car is a manual shifter, the ease with which the clutch engages (or disengages) is a good indication of the attention to detail the manufacturer spent when doing the overall design. Some of the smoothest clutches in the world, by the way, come from Mercedes and Toyota, although not necessarily in that order!

Now you're ready for the serious stuff: acceleration, turning, braking.

Braking is the most difficult function to test without a professional track on which the total stopping distances from "full lock" (all brakes 100% locked) can be properly measured. Since you will not be on a track, simply continue your drive and pay special attention to whether the brakes feel like they're stopping the car "in sync" with your pedal pressure. Poorly designed brakes will always give the impression that they want to take a lot more time to stop the car than you do.

Turning, like braking, is best measured on a professional track with banked turns and an absolute minimum of unfriendly, protruding objects. (If control should be lost on such a track, you really can't do very much damage.) On city streets, a good substitute test is to take corners slightly faster than you ordinarily would, listening carefully for any noises of protest from your tires. If the tires accept your conduct without a murmur, it's a safe bet that the suspension of the car has been well thought out. If, however, the tires start to squeal in protest even at such simple low-speed manoeuvres, the handling and suspension characteristics of the vehicle may leave much to be desired.

Acceleration is relatively easy to assess. Either the car moves as fast as you want it to, or it doesn't. Even cars that boast impressive 0 – 60 statistics in the sales brochure may feel anaemic and underpowered in the real world. The majority of engines in use today are four-cylinder. Still, engines, like people, are not all created equal. Engines of similar displacement (size) can and do perform differently in different chassis when matched to different power-trains and options. Pay special attention here because acceleration is a critical factor for most drivers. If the car feels needlessly sluggish, don't merely deduct points. Pass it by.

On the Highway

Now let's get serious. Move out onto your favourite highway (although not in rush hour, please!). Bring the car up to a respectable cruising speed, close the windows (finally!), and see what happens. If the car shakes, shudders or feels in any way uncomfortable, deduct some more points. Try to carry on a serious conversation with your spouse or pet. Deduct some more points if either of you can't hear what the other person is saying. Turn on the radio and try to decipher the words to the very first song that you hear. If you can't, deduct another point. (Unless, that is, you've tuned into something that's heavy metal, in which case give the car another chance with a station that plays mainly Perry Como and Andy Williams.)

Change lanes a couple of times at cruising speed to simulate an emergency lane change manoeuvre. If the car feels like it wants to wobble or spin, deduct a point. (The technical name for this is "gyroscopic instability." It means the handling and ride characteristics are not up to par.)

While driving straight ahead, use the windows and mirrors to figure out what's happening in all the lanes surrounding you. If you find any blind spots, deduct some more points.

While you're out there, try out the heater and air conditioner. Over many years of tireless testing, we car journalists have determined that heater output should be very hot and air conditioner output very cold. Both units should also perform quietly.

The "Invisibles"

The most complicated part of serious car testing is putting a value on the "invisibles," or the parts of the car that are not objectively quantifiable. Eye appeal is one such factor. The highly successful Taurus/Sable lineup from Ford was originally a source of much unease to the car company because, although it knew the line *performed* well, it wasn't completely sure the public would care for the *styling!* Award or deduct your points as needed. (This is a very subjective thing. Personally, I think the nicest design of all time is the 1968 Mercury Cougar.)

Value for the money is another invisible that is hard to pin down. Sometimes the answer is obvious. The Porsche 911, for example, is a nice car but it costs around $100,000, plus tax. For that kind of money, I can almost buy a small third-world country, so the Porsche definitely loses points in this category. My first test of the VW Fox, on the other hand, revealed not only a spiffy little performer, but an amazing price tag as well. A glance at the Fox's spec sheet confirmed that the car's components were all tried-and-true VW/Audi components being offered at virtually giveaway prices. At the time, I quickly ranked the Fox my best value car of the year.

4

Buying Used

I have never met a used car I didn't like   Robert Appel

"OK, class, how many of you buy cars for status as opposed to basic transportation? In other words, how many of you don't drive your cars — but wear them?"

Of all the questions I ask of my students during the Car Kung Fu course, these two are usually the most vexing.

Truth is, most of us buy cars for the wrong reasons. Or, at least, for reasons other than the most fundamental ones.

How many of us actually do buy cars for reasons other than basic transportation? According to most auto company studies, virtually *all* of us!

In fact, basic transportation, or getting from A to B, is usually *last* on the list of things buyers look for when choosing a vehicle. Instead, criteria such as "look," "image," "interior space," "power" and so on make up an embarrassingly large component of their lists.

Why embarrassing? Because if people purchased cars simply to get from A to B, most of us would drive old Dodge Darts or, failing that, used Toyotas. (No kidding! Surveys recently completed in both the US and Canada rate owner satisfaction with used Toyotas highest among all used car brands over a ten-year period.)

ONE MAN'S OPINION

A really nice letter from a Car Kung Fu student in Wyoming had this comment: "I'm glad about two things. First, that there are new car buyers. Second, that I'm not one of them." The writer went to reminisce about his old '65 Fury, a car that gave him 95,000 almost trouble-free km before a drunk slammed into the car and "totalled" it. Will the new cars deliver the same performance, he asks? Not likely, say I.

It is a basic tenet of Car Kung Fu that one buys and drives a vehicle to get from *A* to *B* as *economically* as possible. Therefore, it follows that a used car, as opposed to a new one, can offer more value for money.

It is not my place to foist my own preferences upon you, the reader. However, may the record show that, although I have driven hundreds of cars and owned or traded dozens, I have purchased new from the friendly neighbourhood new car dealer only once. That was enough, thank you very much.

Looking back, I have mixed memories of the experience. On the plus side, getting into a brand new car — in my case a 1971 VW Fastback with a spiffed-up exhaust system — was a kick. A definite adrenalin high.

But there was a downside. I recall clearly how, once I got the keys to the car, the friendly salesman who, earlier, had been almost ready to marry my sister, completely forgot my name. (This mannerism was later exhibited, in sequence, by the service adviser and all the mechanics who worked on my car. The only one who seemed to recognize me at all was the dealer's cashier.)

I also recall, clearly, how warranty claims which, at the time, I believed to be simple and straightforward became instead deep philosophical issues worthy of the greatest debate. Perhaps even on a par with, "Why are we here?"

I remember that, even though I knew in advance that regular servicings, check-ups, and tune-ups were going to cost me extra, the extra they cost seemed enough for a European vacation. That "checking" the car while the warranty was in place seemed to my unsophisticated sense of mathematics to cost more somehow than actually "fixing" it might.

I also remember, in glowing technicolour, how the fuel-injection system seemed to want to roll over and die within weeks of the warranty's expiring. And how the dealer-applied rust-proofing with the "lifetime guarantee" did not prevent the car from looking pock-marked after only four winters (a matter that was eventually resolved, in my favour, by a sympathetic Small Claims judge).

And, through it all, I remember asking myself the same question over and over: Why?

Why indeed?

Sure, used cars take a bit of work up-front but, to my mind, the costs are generally much more manageable. And predictable.

And if you are thinking, " A used car is someone else's trouble," then you are confusing "used" and "abused."

Leaving aside the delicate question of rust (which will be dissected in a later chapter), the life cycle of the typical motorcar is not what you might expect.

Here are some numbers that may shock and amaze. Almost any rear-drive model built prior to 1985 can usually be kept on the road, safely and reliably, for 15-25 years. The engine alone should deliver anywhere from 175,000 to 250,000 km in its first cycle (before its first rebuild) assuming regular oil changes, valve adjustments and general care. And this is regardless of whether the engine is four-cylinder, eight-cylinder, or six-cylinder.

Think I am kidding? Take the domestic products built between 1968 and 1972 as the high watermark of durability engineering. Properly maintained, those particular vehicles can run for decades. There is a slight decrease in car longevity for cars produced from approximately 1972-1982 and a fairly dramatic decrease from 1985 on.

Even in the most extreme example of short-life-cycle product — front-drive, extensively computerized cars produced since '85 — you should still expect at least 10-12 years, all other things being equal. Since most people keep their vehicles 5-7 years and then trade or sell them for market value, there are millions of vehicles on the road which may give you, the used-car buyer, at least 5 full years of use before it becomes economically unrealistic to keep the machine running.

SOME CARS ARE USED MORE THAN OTHERS

Memorize these basic rules:

- Front engine, rear drive is more durable, less complex, and generally more reliable than front engine, front drive. (Sorry for the tricky terminology, but there *are* mid-engine cars — Fiero, MR2 — and even some rear-engine cars — the Skoda — and I don't want to mix those strange beasties into our discussion!)

- A larger engine (a V-8 or a six-cylinder) will generally be more durable than a four-cylinder. However, this rule is mitigated by the following facts: some manufacturers (Mazda, Toyota, Volvo, Mercedes) have made some extremely solid fours; an engine using aluminium in its construction will be less durable than one that doesn't; regular oil changes and valve adjustments (if needed) are a *must* to keep an engine running to its maximum service life; an engine can be destroyed if left to overheat for only five minutes; and towing anything for any reason will shorten engine life.

- Leaving aside, for the moment, the question of computers, the more electronics — or options, or power-assist features — on the car, the more expensive and troublesome it will be. This means that a car with power steering will cause more trouble than a car without it. A car with air conditioning can be expected to pose a financial nightmare for the overheated owner after about five or six years. A car with power seats, power tailgate, power sunroof and power windows is an economic time bomb waiting to explode in its golden years. And any car with gratuitous power doodads — or extra parts — in its suspension should be avoided at all costs. (The last category includes any car with 4-wheel steering and any car with adjustable or "smart" suspensions.)

   "Aha!" you might be thinking, "surely the author has driven one too many kilometres with his sunroof open. Surely it follows, as night the day, that these power things *add* value to an older car — don't they?" Answer: Only to the uninformed. Whether or not used-car buyers (who have not studied Car Kung Fu) will pay more for these things is secondary. The point is that they cause economic grief later on for whoever owns the car at the time, and that's the bottom line.

- I left the most complex factor for last: those cursed ECMs (Electronic Control Modules) that have worked their way into most cars built since 1985. Although this is not a piece of news that the car makers of the world would like circulated, the sad fact is that the advent of the computerized car has caused a reversal in the durability cycle. Cars today really don't hold up over time. There are two reasons. The first is the cost of maintenance and repair. According to some recent surveys, the number of repairs to the typical modern motorcar has come down with the advent of electronics, whereas the average cost per repair has skyrocketed. This is a direct result of the fact that these ECMs — and the dozens of complex sensors and switches that feed them information every waking moment of your car's life — cannot be repaired, only replaced; and the cost of replacing them is usually in the hundreds, sometimes thousands, of dollars.

And there's more bad news. To appreciate fully how seriously the computer age has reduced the longevity of the typical motorcar, one has to consider for a moment just what is happening to a typical vehicle during those last, precious years of its life, its golden age, so to speak. The springs and shocks may be sagging just a wee bit, the engine response may not be as crisp as in its youth, the car may creak and groan occasionally, and the owner may quickly learn that she has to add oil to the engine on a regular basis to compensate for the normal wear and tear that the rings and valves have been through. In a non-computerized car, however, this is not a problem. The owner may continue driving the car for an extra year or two, confident that she is getting almost a free ride; i.e., that her net depreciation and cost of ownership for those last few thousand kilometres are so low as to be almost a gift.

In a computerized car, however, the computer will quickly notice the change in the exhaust gases caused by the extra oil seeping past the rings, com-pare those numbers with the ones in its memory (a memory programmed when the car was young and new and fresh) and, if it doesn't like the match, it will shut the car down (actually, throw it into something called "limp-in" mode, which is the same thing) until the owner goes out and buys a new $3,000 engine — or scraps the car.

EVERYTHING YOU EVER WANTED TO KNOW ABOUT BUYING USED

What exactly is a used car?

A used car is any car of a year other than the current model year, or any car that has already been registered to one or more owners. It is worth noting that many demonstrators are, in fact, already used or "pre-owned" cars on which a major part of the warranty has already expired. Note also that even a new car is "used" the moment it leaves the showroom with the first owner. If you have doubts, ask the poor consumer who had to return his new car the next day for health reasons how much the dealer gave him for a trade on another new car. Answer: About 20% less than he had paid for the car the day before.

How Much Can You Save Buying Used?

Buckets. Buckets of buckets. First, you save the dreaded "first day" depreciation (sometimes called "first year" although, in fact, the depreciation happens the *moment* the car leaves the showroom). Estimates vary, but first year depreciation swallows up between 20 and 45% of the new car price. Also, a used car will generally trade at its market value, i.e., the measure of what the marketplace thinks it's worth in real life. A new car sells for the dealer list price, i.e., the price the manufacturer thinks it's worth in Wonderland.

What are Used Cars Worth?

Here's some news: Used car "auctions" are held throughout North America every few weeks. Although the public cannot attend, the prices bid here are meant to reflect the prices that the particular makes, models and years will ultimately sell for when turned out onto the retail used car market. More interesting, particular cities can and do generate their own specific used car pricing structures. For example, you may find that a certain car is worth more on the east coast than the west coast, all other factors being equal. The bottom line, therefore, is that the car you are looking at is worth no more and no less than other cars of similar make and use are worth in that specific area! Your first area of attack, therefore, is your own local newspaper. If your tastes are more exotic — or if you live in an area where demand has raised the used car prices to unacceptable levels — you might consider shopping somewhere else and having the car towed or driven back. Be sure the money saved compensates you for your time, though.

"I DID IT MY WAY": SHOPPING OUTSIDE OF HOME

It's true, you don't have to buy a car in your city or town. There are a number of magazines and classified ad services that will put you in touch with buyers out-of-province, out-of-state, or even out-of-country. (*Hemmings* or *Cars and Parts* are two of my favourites — any library will find them for you.) Before you do this, however, consider:

- How will you check out the car? A lot of armchair shoppers have been burned over the years. Just because vendors have a different postal code, doesn't mean they are any more or less honest than the guy down the street.

- How will you ship it? As far as I know, Federal Express still does not have overnight service for cars. Pity. In fact, aside from picking it up yourself, you usually have only two choices. First, you can have the car shipped by a car carrier. Most carriers advertise in the Yellow Pages. Quotes vary so you should shop around. (You will get a better price if the carrier is taking another car or two along the same route as yours.) Or you can approach one of those driveaway services where, for a few dollars up-front, your car will be driven home, depending on your luck, either by a retired clergyman visiting his kin, or by an ex-member of the Manson gang. A note of caution, however: the really old cars, even the classics, will not be accepted as a driveaway because — outside of the person who just purchased it — there may not be many drivers eager to go for a long trip in vintage iron.

As in any other industry, there are *two* price levels. The wholesale is the price a dealer might pay for a particular car in working condition. The retail is the price the dealer might resell that same car for. For specific information, look into the *Blue*, *Red*, or *Black Books* (those are the actual names!) which report on all auction activity in the US and Canada. Your librarian, bank manager, or insurance company can help you locate these books. Surprisingly, you will generally find that the retail spread over wholesale is *not* based on percentage but rather on an average mark-up of about $1,500. (Note also that these reported retail prices are generally *actual* prices not *suggested* — most dealers will ask about $1,000 more for a vehicle than they will actually end up getting. This provides bargaining room!)

Are There Other Benefits to Buying Used?

Absolutely. And you'd be surprised. Used cars have most of the major bugs (warranty repairs) worked out by the previous owner or owners. Used cars, because they represent technology that has been on the market for a while, allow you access to parts and service *other than* those available from the pricey and often unsociable new car dealer. (This is particularly significant on the parts side — quality non-dealer parts from outside sources can save you up to 60% of dealer list. Non-dealer service or labour charges usually result in *additional* savings of about 35%.)

Psychologically, many owners report that used cars make them less paranoid about parking in crowded lots or leaving the car unattended on suspicious-looking streets. Whether or not this sense of security is well founded (studies show that cars selected to be stolen are chosen according to *model* not *year*), there is no denying that owners feel better about leaving their older vehicles to fend for themselves.

What about Make and Model?

Go by the same guidelines you would use to choose a new car but factor in four additional considerations: reliability, cost and availability of parts, complexity of service, and depreciation.

Reliability.

Consumers Reports publishes a Buying Guide issue each year. It includes data on how each type of car has held up since new. These statistics are further broken down according to the various mechanical subsystems within the car itself. An overall desirability rating for the vehicle is also given. Back issues are available from the magazine's publisher and at most libraries.

CHASING THE MARKET

It does not make sense to buy when the market is severely out of balance, when demand far exceeds supply. Here, from my diary, is my own experience in 1988 trying to buy a used car, quickly, in a demand-heavy market:

Zipping through dozens of ads, I quickly target a '72 Toyota Celica at $1,900 with very low mileage. A 30-minute conversation with the owner confirms that I have indeed struck pay dirt: the vehicle is garage-stored, rust-free, and even has a file folder chock full of old maintenance records. Even better, the owner lives a mere 12 minutes from my place. Literally. "Don't even breathe," I say, "I'm already there." I make the trip in 9 minutes flat, slowing only for stop-lights and gravity. The owner's younger brother greets me at the door. "The car was just sold," he announces between bubble gum chews. "Sorry," he adds. But he is just being polite. He isn't the one who is truly sorry; I am. By that after-noon, I discover to my horror that in my local market over 50% of all used cars are being sold on the first day their ad appears.

More adventures the next day. An ad for an '82 Mazda 626, fully loaded, no rust, practically jumps off the page. The owner drops hints that he has had the car for years and hates to part with it. He wants $3,500 — $500 more than market value. That is not necessarily a bad thing. Often a really good car lists for more because the owner knows just how great the vehicle really is. Thinking my luck is changing, I show up at the owner's house at 7:00 in the morning. No time for small talk. I suggest taking the car for a test drive and then, once behind the wheel, make a beeline for my mechanic. "Since we're already here, you don't mind if I check a few things out?" I ask innocently. The owner mumbles something that sounds like a "Yes." In 10 minutes, over $1,000 worth of problems have come to light. Leaky rear cylinders, bad bearings, missing engine parts, and an assortment of electrical oddities. "The car was safety-certified," mumbles the owner in a voice that seems to be losing conviction by the minute. "It shouldn't have been," retorts my trusty mechanic. The car owner seems to take the news badly. (Later I find out why: my mechanic got a very agitated phone call from the car's original owner. Turned out the car had been sold just the week before for $2,500. The fellow I was dealing with, the new owner, had been trying for a "quick flip," and was surprised to discover, in the process, that he was the one who had been taken!)

Back to the classifieds. I don't know the meaning of the word "quit." (In fact, there are lot a of words I don't know the meaning of.) The next morning I drive 90 minutes to an out-of-the-way suburb to see a '72 model Toyota that is "In excellent condition, dealer maintained, dealer certified, dealer rust-proofed and oil undercoated." The directions are difficult and I get lost three times. I console myself with the thought that I could be first potential buyer to make it this far. In fact, I am so far off the beaten track I could found a village, build a cabin and settle. I finally find the correct address. The car beckons seductively from the driveway. Bad news. On the phone I had asked the owner what the body was like. "A little rust over the fenders," he had said. Sure, pal, tell me another. Looking the car over, I find large pockets of rust that will turn the car to swiss cheese within another 12 months. That ad takes on new meaning. Clearly, the owner had turned to oil undercoating only after he'd realized how useless the dealer stuff had been. I hear footsteps behind me. The owner misinterprets my look of shock as unfettered desire. "Don't forget the price is firm," he announces. On the long drive home I mentally list the 4,008 snappy responses I could have made to that remark, but didn't... .

One last try and then I bike to work. I spot an ad for an-other '82 Mazda 626 on the very first day it appears in the Star. I catch the owner on the phone just as he comes in the door for dinner. He gives me directions. "I'm on my way over," I tell him. I fight rush hour traffic to arrive at his house before 6:00 p.m. "You're the first one," he tells me. "Darn right," I reply. The car looks well kept. I read the owner his rights. "I will buy this car from you right now for the advertised price," I say. "No bargaining. But the car is subject to mechanical in-spection. If my mechanic says it has problems, I get my money back. OK?"

The owner agrees. I hand-write a sale memo and he signs. We arrange a visit to my mechanic for the next day. That night he gets 18 calls for the car. He tells everyone the car is sold. The next morning Mike the Mechanic checks out the car, and likes it. I am now the proud owner of an '82 Mazda 626 in fairly respectable shape. And I hope it lasts at least 100 years, because that's how long it will be before I'll feel like shopping for another used car in a seller's market.

Cost and Availability of Parts

Be careful here. The muffler system to be installed in a used Mercedes can cost as much as an *entire* used Hyundai! Once again, *Consumer Reports* is a good place to start. Also have a look at back issues of *Popular Science*. Each month that magazine publishes the typical cost of a parts basket for each car they test. If, for example, headlamps and brake pads on a particular make cost double the price of the same parts on the others, avoid that car! Availability is another issue entirely. Generally, parts for virtually any Japanese or American car (or Japan-US hybrid, in most cases) are readily available from both dealer *and* non-dealer sources — an important consideration in view of the significant cost saving that comes from successfully circumventing the dealer. Many European cars, unfortunately, cannot make the same claim. Also, avoid cars that have only recently come to market (like Hyundai). Parts availability is strange, to say the least.

Complexity of Service

This is not as much a function of make or model as of *design* itself. Clearly, a car with 4-wheel drive, turbo-charging, a computerized self-adjusting suspension, and 4-wheel steering (Yes! These do exist on the same car!) will be a major nightmare for any owner other than a professional mechanic, and a minor nightmare for him.

Depreciation

Published studies of depreciation, although they exist, are hard to find. Here's what I do: I get hold of a *Blue, Red,* or *Black Book* (as above) and locate, among the wholesale/ retail auction data, the *original suggested list price* for the base model. Then, for the preceding five years, I calculate:

$$\frac{\text{original list} - \text{current wholesale for the year} \times 100}{\text{original list}}$$

Averaging your results over five years yields a good indication of expected depreciation.

Is There a *Best* Used Car?

How many angels can dance on the head of a pin? (First you answer my question, then I'll answer yours!) We could talk about this one for hours. As I mentioned above, you may want to choose rear drive over front drive — if you can. You should avoid strange technology as much as possible. And — I don't own any stock in the company by the way — you should look at a Toyota first. In a long series of studies done in the US and Canada, the overall durability rating of Toyota, from the present going back almost 20 years, is the highest of all cars — all things being equal. If you want to play the odds, play Toyota. Toyotas depreciate slowly, are easy to fix, are well built and reliable, and have a plentiful and reasonable parts supply. In all these categories, they tend to outperform other used cars. Other winners include Mazda, Nissan and Mercedes Benz.

Where Do you Buy the Best Used Cars?

Wherever you like. A used-car dealer seems the most obvious choice. All the powerful Car Kung Fu self-defence techniques from Chapter 3 apply to buying from a dealer. The only other tip to keep in mind is that it is preferable, when dealing with a dealer, to buy the car before it has been "detailed."

DETAILING

Used-car dealers are not dummies. Over a hundred years or so they have figured out that the car's *perceived* value is much more important than its actual value. And that they can greatly enhance a car's perceived value by spending a few hundred dollars on detailing — doing cosmetic touch-ups which hide blemishes and cover up imperfections. This includes obvious things like brush-on paint, waxing and cleaning. It also includes less obvious and quite devious things like varnishing rubber to make it look new, steam cleaning parts to hide evidence of leaks, selectively rust-proofing the underside to give the impression the entire car was rust-treated, and so on. Detailing stinks. It costs the dealer money (which must be recouped) and it hides the true condition of the car. Try to avoid it.

A used car from a private owner is likely to be a better deal, provided the private person is the original owner and has the old work orders to prove it. (If the owner seems to know less about the car than you do, and can't explain recent mechanical work, pass the vehicle by. Something is not kosher in Kansas.) After buying and selling a handful of cars over the years, I have come to prefer to buy from an owner who is only minimally car-literate because such an owner is more likely to leave the car's maintenance to a pro. A more car-literate owner will too often be tempted to save money by doing home repairs. In this hi-tech era of ours, that almost always means trouble. (Special bargaining tip in dealing with private sellers: "Yes, your price is quite fair for a car in good working condition and ordinarily I'd love to pay it. However, my mechanic has found the following repairs which must be done to the car immediately to make it safe and reliable. If you deduct these repairs from your price, I think we have a deal." This works all the time!)

OOPS — WATCH OUT FOR ...

Remember those bananas in the crankcase? In the old days fruit would be added to a badly worn and noisy engine to quieten it down. The car wouldn't last any longer, but it sure would be easier to sell! Today, folks don't need to stop at the grocery to accomplish this. There are a half-dozen additives and thickeners sold commercially which do the same thing. They catch the unwary buyer off-guard and make the vendor a happier person. But the car will still need engine work down the road, and its cold-weather starting will be seriously impaired. How to prevent being caught by bananas in the crankcase? A pro can feel the oil and tell if it is doctored. As a regular buyer, the only sure-fire test is to have the oil changed at your own expense, then perform your test drive.

An even more common trick is to "quickie paint" a rust-bucket, covering the rust and making the car look great for at least a few months. The economics here are staggering. A $500 paint job can add as much as $2,000 to the perceived value of a used car. However, for $500 you get little or no rust repair, so, when the rust bubbles through promptly thereafter, the $500 seems almost a complete waste — except for the seller, that is, who made fast cash on the deal. How to spot the quickie paint job? First, determine if the car has been recently painted by looking at the finish. A fresh paint job is usually obvious. If in doubt, cross-check by looking for overspray on trim and black rubber. Another tip: If the car was ever rust-proofed, it will have black rust-proofing plugs, about the size of a dime. If the plugs are painted over, they are a dead giveaway the car has been recently repainted.

Next, stick your head under the rear gas tank with a flashlight and look for rust. This area is the best indicator I have found of the true rust condition of a car. If the underside is all rusty and corroded, but the paint looks wonderful, you are probably on a one-way ticket to Bilksville. Also, run your fingers over the body looking for slight ridges and bumps. Rust doesn't like new paint, and imperfections in the work will begin to show as early as a few weeks after the cover-up. If you have a magnet, and a lot of patience, touch the magnet over different spots on the body, trying to feel areas which the magnet doesn't seem to grab as much. Those areas are either severely rusted or damaged from an accident (see below). In either case, this is not a car you want to get to know better. If you come up with nothing on these tests, but your gut tells you something is not quite right, consider paying a body shop a fast $20 to look over the car and give you an opinion. In my experience, body shops will do this not so much for the money as for the chance to criticize someone else's work!

Another little trick you want to watch out for is the "out of sight, out of mind" game some owners play with the gauges. All cars are designed so that all the warning lights activate just before the engine is started. This means that as the key is turned you should see, at the least,

- an ENGINE or CHECK ENGINE light;
- an OIL PRESSURE gauge;
- an ALTERNATOR warning light;
- a TEMPERATURE warning light.

It is not unheard of for a seller to disconnect a gauge or two, prior to selling, to hide a problem!

And, finally, avoid the used car that has been in a serious accident. To check for recent evidence of an accident, follow virtually the same guidelines as for the quickie paint job above. If your magnet doesn't want to stick at all to a major portion of the body, then the car has been in a major fender-bender. Examine very closely the electrical connectors under the hood and in the trunk; they are a reliable indicator of recent body work due to collision. (New wiring, or lots of splices, is the giveaway.)

Reliable used cars are also to be found at fleet auctions (large companies selling off their fleets to the public), car rental agencies, and even police or custom impound lots.

How Do You Check Out a Used Car?

No, I never promised you a rose garden. If I make the check out process appear easier than it is, you will almost certainly have trouble later on with the parts I neglected to tell you about! If I make the whole thing more complex than necessary, you will come to dread the very notion of spending great amounts of time and money on each vehicle you consider. So, instead, let me share with you the compromise check-out program which is at the core of Car Kung Fu. Using this method, you perform a short and simple list of simple checks on your own. If the car passes these simple tests, and you still like it, *then you go to your chosen mechanic* (Chapter 5) to check out the things I have listed below. It doesn't matter whether you understand completely these more detailed tests. All that matters is that you insist your mechanic check them out and report on them. The report itself, along with a detailed estimate for each repair, will be explanation enough. *Do not* leave the selection of tests to the discretion of the mechanic. In these situations, even honest wrench-turners tend to undercheck at the time to save money, knowing that, if they miss something, you'll be back later on to have the repair made anyway.

On your own:

1. Inspect the car visually for signs of recent repainting. (If it has been repainted, there will *always* be signs of overspray on the rubber or chrome trim, no

matter how professional the job.) Since most used cars are painted merely to hide problems, very recent repainting should be a negative sign or, at the least, something to investigate carefully.

2. Check for rust by looking under the rear of the car, around the back wheels, with a flashlight. The true rust condition of the car will be revealed here, and often in the bottom seams of the doors.

3. Check for major body repair by running a magnet over the shell. Where the magnet will not stick, you have putty. Where you have putty, you have a problem.

4. Unless the front tires are brand new, uneven wear patterns can indicate potential front-end problems. Simply compare the left with the right and draw your own conclusions.

5. Find out where the car is usually parked (usually not a difficult bit of detective work) and see what precious fluids are leaking from what areas. Note these findings for your mechanic to follow-up on later, if the car gets to that stage.

6. Open the hood and make a note of any excessively shiny parts (newly changed — why?) or excessively wet parts (what is *leaking* and what will it cost to fix?).

7. Go for a test drive after carefully instructing the owner (sitting next to you) to keep quiet so you can listen to the engine. Even if you are not an expert on engine noises (most of us aren't), keeping the owner quiet saves her from having to lie to you about each of the car's quirks and, in so doing, risking her soul to possible eternal perdition. A proper engine is a symphony of sound, and no one repetitive noise should rise above the rest.

PRIVATE SALE?

Why bother selling your own car at all when that nice friendly dealer down the block will take it off your hands for a song? Because it's the *wrong* song, that's why — car dealers make a minimum of about $1,000 on every used car they deal, so whatever price you are offered, you can be sure it's at least $1,000 too little!

On the other hand, there *are* some pitfalls in selling your own car which you should be aware of. First, with all that traffic coming to look at your car, expect a few oddballs in the bunch. Not the sort you would want a friend to date, for instance. Furthermore, unless you are very careful how you handle the paperwork when actually completing the sale, these same people may come *back* to visit you the first time the car fails to perform properly. Or you may just find yourself in Small Claims Court, which amounts to the same thing.

So here's what you do: unless you actually are a top mechanic, explain clearly that you know absolutely nothing about cars but you think your car runs OK. In that way, you can't be caught making any statements which might later be interpreted as misleading. Mark clearly on the bill of sale, "No warranty or guarantee of any kind" and make sure you get a xerox copy for yourself. Never let a stranger drive away alone in your car if the registration and insurance are still in your name. A certified cheque is nice but cash is nicer. Believe it or not, a certified cheque can be stopped. It doesn't happen often, but once is more than enough. If you take a deposit, specify in writing that the deposit is forfeit if the buyer doesn't finish the transaction. If you don't specify this, the buyer can not only change his mind, but he can ask for his money back also. If the buyer tries to bargain you down by listing all the defects in the car, remind him that it is, after all, a used car to start with. If it were a brand new car you would be asking a lot more, wouldn't you? Finally, pricing. When you price the car, never mind all those silly black and red books everyone talks about. The car should be priced at its fair value in your trading area. You can determine this by looking in the local paper and seeing what similar models are going for. Good luck!

If you still want the car, take your notes from your own check to your mechanic. Request a written report on the following, which will cost about $40-$60 (not a lot of money when you consider what buying the wrong car could cost).

1. Rad pressure test (for rad leaks).

2. Visual underbody inspection of exhaust, and suspension check.

3. Compression and cylinder balance tests (next best thing to a chest X-ray of your engine). Remember: you don't have to know how to do these tests; simply how to ask to have them done!

4. R & R (remove and replace) all four wheels to check brakes. Over the last decade brake repair costs have skyrocketed; check all four wheel systems before making a decision.

5. Front-end inspection on a 4-wheel alignment machine. Note that you are not asking for an actual 4-wheel alignment, which is costly, but the pre-check, which is much simpler. The pre-check can spot major frame damage that might otherwise go undetected.

6. Exhaust gas analysis. Once again, you are not asking for a tune-up (expensive) but only the pre-check. This can spot serious troubles with the on-board computer or ignition/fuel systems. At the least, it can catch a severely neglected engine.

As I said earlier, a well maintained car can give a lot of service. For example, I purchased a '72 Pontiac Lemans in '75 and gave it away to a young student in 1988 because I didn't have enough garage space for all my other cars. My used '78 Mazda GLC, which I use during winter, still has an almost original engine compartment. In 1989, a reporter for the *Toronto Star*, to prove a point, bought a 20-year-old

Mercedes in Victoria, BC, and immediately drove it thousands of kilometres through the mountains and over the prairies to Toronto. According to the latest information, car and driver are both reported in excellent condition.

What about Parts and Service for Older Cars?

For popular makes there is usually a plentiful parts supply in the aftermarket ("non-dealer" suppliers) for about 15-25 years. After that you may have to contact suppliers who specialize in older cars. They usually advertise in magazines like *Cars and Parts* or *Hemmings*. Keep in mind that, at this writing, it is entirely possible to get almost any mechanical part for most domestic cars produced back into the 1950s — a statistic that bodes well for used cars of future years also.

CAN YOU MAKE MONEY WITH A USED CAR?

You can, but it requires effort. By picking a "hot" model before it becomes hot, you can sell your car after years of use for as much as, or more than, you paid originally. This feat, which sometimes requires the services of a professional clairvoyant, would have had you pick up, for example certain Honda and VW models (Prelude and the Bug Convertible, respectively) just before the market fell in love with them. Generally speaking, however, this is a sticky business because a car with inherent collector or snob value must be in above-average condition with very low mileage. Another problem with these cars is that your own insurance might not be doing the car justice. You could lose money if the car was stolen or damaged and your insurer gave you only depreciated value. If this sounds like your situation, talk to an independent insurance broker now!

5

Mastering Mechanics

This, most certainly, is the point in the book where you expect me to tell you what rotten, nasty and greedy people mechanics are.

I have absolutely no intention of doing that. Instead, let me give you a few reasons why no sane, intelligent person in today's world might ever want to become a car mechanic:

- High complexity. Whereas a computer or electronic technician has *only* to understand electronics, today's mechanic has to be adept also at diagnosing — everything from a bad oxygen sensor (fully electronic) to a bad ball joint (fully mechanical).

- High change, high stress. Cars are changing from year to year, faster than any piece of known technology other than, perhaps, the computer. And the reason for that one limitation is simply that cars *use* computers extensively themselves. In a society that has trouble getting doctors and lawyers to take refresher courses, how can we expect mechanics to take time off the job regularly to find out what they've been missing?

- Low pay. For equal or superior skill levels, a mechanic gets paid less than a carpenter, plumber or electrician. This fact is entirely without dispute.

THE VIEW FROM THE OTHER SIDE

You are a certified, properly trained car mechanic. You spent more time learning your craft than a plumber or electrician would, yet somehow you are making less money. Also, plumbing and electricity hasn't changed much in the last century, but under-hood automotive technology seems to be changing from week to week. You've just put in a hard day's work and you really would like to go home. But you can't. Waiting behind your counter is Ms. Watchamacallit, the lady who brought in that dead car at 7:00 a.m. this morning and glared at you as though it was all somehow *your* doing. You spent four hours diagnosing the problem and finally determined that it was all the fault of the *last* mechanic she took the car to! You don't look forward to explaining to her that not only does she lose all the money she put into *that* job but also, to set things right, you had to do the same job all over again. You realize that you would rather be anywhere else than in this situation right now. She tells you that she would rather be having a root canal than fight with you over your bill, and you tell her you feel exactly the same way!

- Dangerous working conditions. The conditions mechanics are exposed to on the job are hazardous. They have to inhale engine fumes, work (until recently, anyway) with asbestos brake parts, handle carcinogenic fluids (oil, rad waste) and play hide-'n-seek under a two-tonne piece of metal that is often supported by only a hand jack.

- High cost of tools. Most mechanics are expected to bring their *own* tools to work. These days, the tools necessary to work on a given car can cost anywhere from $5-$5,000.

- No respect. There was a time, about a million years ago, when certain trades or occupations attracted people because they had inherent prestige. (Letter carrying was one of these. My, how times change!) Mechanics used to enjoy working on cars to make them better, and then talking to owners to let them know what they had done. Today's mechanics are lucky if they can make the car run, let alone run better. And most shops keep the mechanic and the customer as far apart as possible, substituting instead a service adviser, whose best advice often concerns possible methods of payment.

- Monopolistic pricing. The industry evolution described in Chapter 2 has had negative effects for mechanics as well as consumers. Just as consumers no longer have the choice of where to go to get parts, so mechanics all too often find themselves ordering parts from the original manufacturer. What is not realized, however, is that parts from the original manufacturer cost the most (as a rule) for both mechanics and consumers. The only one that comes out on top is the manufacturer.

All in all, the mechanics trade is not one I would choose voluntarily, particularly not in this "me first" world of ours. By no simple coincidence, the supply of mechanics throughout North America is at an all-time low, while demand is at an all-time high.

If you watch the TV commercials, you might get the impression that the service trade is nothing but a bunch of smiling young men in clean coveralls who have your car fixed, cleaned and ready by the time you arrive.The reality is quite different.

Consider this scene. You bus to your service shop to see how that $75 tune-up for your batmobile is going, and are presented with a bill for $400 and change. When you delicately probe the issue with the stoic cashier, she points out that there are seven other equally perturbed people waiting in line for their vehicles. As you glumly reach for your plastic, you finally understand the term "five o'clock surprise."

TWO MANY SHOPS SPOIL THE ENGINE

A car owner decided to put a brand new engine in her five year old domestic sedan. Not a new engine, exactly. A rebuilt one, which is almost like new. After doing her homework, the owner decided to get her rebuilt engine from a major retail chain store. The cost of the new hardware was almost $2,000, and that didn't include installation. But keep in mind that most of us have trouble changing a car fuse, yet alone an engine. So the owner went and asked a private garage to make the switch for her. That was another $700 or so. Now, almost $3,000 later, the owner is in a pretty good mood because she now has a vehicle with a brand new engine for a fraction of the cost of a new car.

Then trouble strikes. The engine coughs, runs rough, shakes, burns oil and, generally, uses a lot of gas. Several trips to the garage that installed the engine do *not* produce results. The owner then comes to the obvious conclusion: the new engine was "defective." She gets on the phone to that national chain store and yells bloody murder. The chain store people want to help but first they have a simple request. "Have the engine examined by our mechanic before we refund your money," they say, "just to make sure the installation was done right." That special mechanical inspection, however, reveals that the engine was installed very poorly. Wires were not connected, pieces were lost, and a special valve in the choke system was jammed, making the engine run incorrectly and use a lot of extra fuel.

Now the motorist is between a rock and a hard place. The shop that did the installation blames the engine and the engine people blame the shop. And now the second shop, the one that did the "inspection," wants to be paid for its time. Our owner is not a happy woman. I rechecked all the facts in this story personally for the owner and came to the conclusion that the problem really was the installation. Since the owner chose the installation garage herself, and the bad installation damaged the new engine, the real fault probably lay with that first garage. But a lot of time had passed, the first garage denied everything, and there was no real proof to go on. I felt badly for the owner, but there was not much that could be done after the fact. Here is the Car Kung Fu tip: Whenever you buy any major car part, have the installation done by the same people that sell you the part. In this case, the owner should have let the chain store do the full installation, regardless of cost. And, if the people who sell the part don't want to install, then buy your parts somewhere else. It's that simple.

Another scene: You've just shelled out $20 for a taxi to take you to the garage where Old Reliable is being attended to. Lately, Old Reliable hasn't been living up to its nickname. It's been losing power on hills, stalling at stop lights, and rattling the fillings in your back teeth whenever you take it over 90 km/h. As you step up to the counter to ask what the damages are, you suddenly realize that you've stepped into the automotive equivalent of the Twilight Zone. A voice inside your head tells you your bill will almost definitely be higher than you thought. You will have no idea what the items listed on the invoice are referring to. The car will run more or less as it always did. And the young man behind the counter is looking at you just like your third-grade teacher used to when you had trouble remembering what day of the week it was. You walk into the service garage and, sure enough, that's exactly the way things happen....

And still another: You love your new car outrageously. Price is no object in affairs of the heart — so off to the dealer you go for everything: repairs, service, maintenance, even oil changes. Oops! Now there is an unfamiliar light on the dash advising you that your anti-lock brake system is on the fritz, and the earliest appointment you can get from the dealer is a full three weeks away! Talk about a friend in need! Where do you go for repairs? And what will you use for brakes in the meanwhile?

KNOW THY CAR

The "knowing" we are talking about here, while not quite biblical, is still a peculiar sort of knowing. It is somewhere between the in-depth mechanical understanding that might come from, for example, taking a night course — and the spiritual, almost ethereal, understanding that arises from, say, meditating on your fuel injectors for a few hours. This is the sort of knowledge that one gleans with age and experience. To illustrate: After a few bad experiences with prematurely worn-out tires, you might learn to say to your mechanic, "The alignment on this car has been weak since the day I bought it. Please check it *now*, before a problem develops, rather than later." Interestingly, one of the best (and most ignored) sources of knowledge for your car is other people who happen to drive the same make and model. No kidding. The next time you see someone driving the same car you have, hop over, introduce yourself, and discreetly ask if any of the mechanical bits and pieces have been especially trouble-prone lately. Once armed with these valuable nuggets of information, you can ask your mechanic to check the same bits on your car *before* trouble happens!

What these all too familiar episodes tell us is that being a car owner today is no picnic either. While fancy gadgets and doodads on new machines abound ("memory seats" or "heated mirrors" anyone?), maintenance costs have tended to increase along with mechanical complexity.

To top it off, the car makers of the world insist upon using the paying public as a kind of living laboratory, turning out imperfect designs which look great on paper but fail miserably in the real world. It is left to the hapless owner to find someone whom she can entrust with the job of setting things right. And that choice is far from easy.

One of the basic principles of Car Kung Fu is that average consumers pay about double what they should for service. And, of course, that the amount spent can be shaved dramatically by following the simple principles of the book.

But, let me emphasize again, nothing here says that the mechanics are primarily to blame. There are some outright cheats, sure. But I estimate that for every outright cheat wielding a wrench, there are ten mechanics who simply don't have a clue as to what they are doing. These are the guys keeping food out of your mouth.

To save money you need to:

- Learn about your car — what it needs, and what it doesn't.
- Learn about mechanics — how to talk to them.
- Learn about the different shops that offer to service your cars — what each does best, and worst.
- Finally, learn how to find a handful of good mechanics — and stick with them.

How your car works — and the work it needs on a regular basis — is discussed in the next chapter.

RATCHETING THE RETRO-ROCKETS: THE SECRET LANGUAGE OF CAR MECHANICS

The language mechanics speak is important, and is something you should learn. It won't help you order a meal in a foreign restaurant, but it will save you enough to be able to go there in the first place!

Learn the syntax of car repair. Unlike motorists, who assume that cars break down because the planets are in the wrong position, mechanics are trained to believe that everything happens for a reason. You can work with them, rather than against them, by catering to this belief.

It really is not hard. Remember how, when the washing machine broke down last summer, you made those gurgle-gurgle noises over the phone so the nice repair person could better understand what had happened? Car mechanics expect the same thing! Before bringing your car in, make a list of the following things:

1. What the problem is, in simple terms. Don't try to "out-guess" the mechanic by saying clever things like, "Needs a tune-up" or "Change the hydro-fibulutor." Trying to out-guess your mechanic is about as expensive a hobby as commodity trading. Some might even say more expensive.

2. Under what circumstances does the problem arise? Accelerating or slowing down? Uphill or downhill? When the engine is cold or warmed up? Summer or winter? In the rain? Full load? Just after filling up? Be specific.

3. If the car was recently in another shop for any reason at all, bring all receipts. Similarly, if any well-intentioned member of your family was do-it-yourselfing on the car over a peaceful Saturday afternoon, find out what exactly was done and tell the mechanic about that also.

4. Are there any unusual sounds or smells associated with the problem? Don't be shy. Describe. The mechanic will understand immediately what you are talking about. For example, valve problems sound like there is a giant alarm clock under the hood; an overheating transmission smells like someone is cooking a pair of rubber galoshes on your engine; warped discs make braking seem like you are driving over beer cans, etc.

5. Are there any new drivers using the car? If the brakes started to wear quickly just after your teen-

ager starting driving, you may have solved the mystery before you even get to the mechanic!

6. Any unusual circumstances in the car's use? Mainly highway driving? Lots of stop-and-go city driving? Mention that as well. (One of the classic stories in the car repair business concerns a gentleman who was always bringing his car in for a manual brake adjustment because the automatic adjusting mechanism never seemed to work properly. The automatic mechanism, by the way, is designed to adjust the brakes whenever the car is driven in reverse. After months of investigation, the mechanic discovered that the owner lived in a house with a circular driveway so that, in effect, the car was never driven in reverse, not even for a short time!)

Finally, it wouldn't hurt to memorize a few "foreign phrases" that mechanics use, so that you can converse on their level, if only for a moment or two:

R & R   *Remove and Replace. This usually accompanies the replacement of a hard-to-reach part. For example, to replace the timing chain, a $50 part, you might first have to R & R the engine, itself a $500 job.*

Adjust   *These days very few parts on the car are adjustable, so thank your lucky stars if something on your vehicle was adjusted instead of replaced. We still adjust valves, for example.*

Overhaul   *An innocuous looking word that can cost you big bucks. To overhaul a system or subsystem (e.g, rear brakes) you have to replace every part in that system that is worn or partly worn. Ouch! (On the other hand, overhauling an individual component, such as a distributor, is not as complex or expensive.)*

Tune   *Watch out for this word! Modern cars are no longer tunable. All critical specifications are factory-set. If your mechanic uses this word, it's time to find a new mechanic.*

Emission System   *A catch-all meaning any part directly or indirectly related to the emission system. The reason this is such an important concept is that all parts of this system are, by law, covered by a factory warranty that far exceeds the normal warranty given with the car. If it's an emission part that needs work, you might get it repaired free at the dealer!*

Calibrate   *Seems just a fancier version of "adjust," doesn't it? In fact, certain electronic parts of the newer cars require calibration when they are installed.*

Diagnose   *Aha! Another $50-an-hour word. Almost all parts of the modern car are so heavily computerized that diagnosis — which used to be almost free — can take as much or more time than the repair itself. Don't be surprised if today's technician actually wants to get paid for this time!*

Reset   *There are many warning systems on the car. If one activates, and you bring the car in for service, the technician will have to reset the system.*

Cut or Turn   *Brake work is so specialized that it has its own peculiar vocabulary. Certain parts can be reused if put on a lathe and smoothed out.*

Drain and fill   *Many systems of the car are still more or less fluid-dependent. These include, usually, engine, transmission, clutch reservoir, radiator, axle, brakes and steering components.*

SHOPPING FOR A SHOP

There are many types of service facilities feverishly competing for your automotive dollar. Each has its pros and cons. Consider:

The Dealer

In theory, the dealer has the most up-to-date equipment and the mechanics are the most skilled in working with your particular make and model.

Sound too good to be true? That may be the case. In fact, the dealer often uses the service end of the business as a profit centre, to balance the budget when new car sales are sluggish. The dealer's overhead is staggering. Parts and service tend, overall, to cost more here than anywhere else. Also, most dealer parts are inventoried and priced by computer, so price increases — even on older, in-stock parts — can arrive daily or even hourly, depending on the programming! True, the dealer does have access to all that shiny new diagnostic equipment from the manufacturer, but is under no legal compulsion, generally, to buy any of it! And dealer mechanics take home only a fraction of the posted shop rate (the dealer keeps the rest), so employee morale may be poor at best. Finally, needless parts sales are often encouraged by commissions, and overall staff turnover tends to be higher than the trade average.

Also — an endless source of consternation for drivers — you never really get a chance to meet your mechanic! All too often, an excessively pleasant fellow in a white smock (with "Service Adviser" neatly stenciled in blue on the front) will act as go-between for you. His manner is designed to convey the impression that he may be a mechanic himself, but, generally, he isn't. In fact, he may be no more than a glorified salesperson who earns commissions (in addition to his regular draw) for any extra repair procedures he can sell you. To top it off, getting in the bay doors at most dealerships these days requires an appointment! Fine, if you are not in a rush, but what do you do if the problem is critical?

Franchised (national) "generalist" shops

These are nationally known chains, such as Firestone or Goodyear, that will attempt most types of repair on your car.

Here volume purchasing power does pay off — sort of. Usually these shops do a brisk counter trade in specialty parts (tires, for example) and run the service section merely as an adjunct. Pressure to stay both friendly and competitive works in your favour, and head office's constant paranoia about bad publicity will ensure things remain liveable. Still, unlike the dealer, they offer no guarantee their mechanics are fully capable of working on your car! More critically, these facilities are pretty popular and, generally, won't think twice about turning away any job that seems difficult or awkward. Also, franchise shops with fixed rate specials — "Brakes for $49.95" — have been found to more likely than any other service facility to overcharge or "bait and switch" the consumer. The reason? At those prices there isn't enough profit left on the table to buy toilet paper for their washrooms, let alone carry their ad budgets. They may advertise a service for $49.95, but when your car comes in for an estimate, the price will suddenly shoot up to $249.95.

Franchise (national) "specialty" shops

These are nationally known chains, such as AAMCO, that limit themselves to one type of repair only, such as brakes, mufflers or transmissions.

Tread cautiously. If you go, for example, to a transmission shop with what later turns out to be an ignition problem, you'll get your tranny fixed *anyway*. Whether you needed it or not! The same can be said about brake, front-end and muffler specialists. They do what they do. Period. The *good news*? If your problem really is in the tranny, or brakes, or whatever, then these guys will likely know just what to do to get Old Reliable humming again! In the case of most vehicles built since 1985, for example, there is a tonne of evidence that certain problems that seem to originate with the engine can, in fact, be caused by the transmission, and vice versa. It takes a top diagnostician to tell the difference. However, should you frequent a shop that specializes in only one (or the other) of these areas, it is unlikely that anything other than the shop's speciality will be offered.

Diagnostic Clinics

From the mechanic's viewpoint, there is little or no money in 100%-labour diagnostic work. The real dollars are made in the service end, where specific operations can be charged by a flat rate, and also in parts sales. Mark-ups here sometimes reach 60-80%. Ergo, it can be argued that there is no profit in buying and maintaining thousands of dollars' worth of diagnostic equipment unless you use same to find problems with customers' cars. Problems that you, yourself, want to be selected for in order to set things right. Consider also that there is no such animal as a perfectly running car *anyway*. Every vehicle will, in time, develop quirks and quarks that may show up as abnormalities in a detailed diagnosis but, practically, will leave performance quite unimpaired. In this light, these shops are an invitation to possible financial mayhem.

The Friendly Corner Filling Station...

Really isn't quite so friendly anymore. Chances are the oil company that owns the land has converted to self-serve and has leased the service bays to an independent freelance operator who may or may not be around next month to stand by the work done this month. If, on the other hand, the service area is run by the same operator who runs the pumps, and that operator has been there a while (and the lease has some time left to run), then you may just be in luck. These steadier stations depend heavily on customer loyalty and repeat business. What they lack in raw skill they may make up for in zeal. A tried-and-true corner garage is not a bad choice.

One final tip: Avoid garages that stand alone in their area or on an exceptionally busy intersection. Monopoly pricing will tempt the former, and a high volume of transient business will discourage the latter from worrying about long-term customer satisfaction.

The "Last Chance" Garages (Independents)

This is truly the last hope for the practitioner of Car Kung Fu. These guys can't coast along on counter sales of tires or mufflers, they don't pump gas between jobs, and they sure can't rely on national advertising to lure the inquisitive into their bays. It's perform or perish. Word of mouth, return business, and happy/smiley customers are their mainstay. To keep things tickedyboo, the really good ones will read technical manuals in their spare time, competitively shop for parts among a wide variety of suppliers, and bend over backwards to keep prices within reason. I've even known independents, on their own initiative, call a junk yard for a customer's part when they felt the item was being overpriced as new! Mind you, independents are not just saints. There are sinners as well. But you can spot the good guys by checking for (a) recommendations from business with large fleets, like pizza shops, or police garages; (b) a good store of up-to-date diagnostic equipment and repair manuals; and (c) an owner who talks to *you* directly instead of hiding behind a counter or white smock.

GOOD ADVICE!

A recent polling of almost 3,000 consumers who went to get their cars fixed in the San Francisco area produced some unexpected results. Overall, according to the survey conducted by the *Bay Area Consumers Checkbook,* higher-priced repair shops received lower ratings than their lower-priced counterparts. This finding is critical — that price is not the issue to look at when choosing a mechanic. Quality and reputation are far more important. In fact, as the consumers in San Francisco noted, a shop with modern premises, fancy equipment and a high advertising budget really may be a shop that has to charge the most, just to break even. The survey noted that the average price quoted to get a heater core replaced in a 1983 Ford Escort varied from $135 to $500. That means the highest price for the job was more than three times the lowest. Ouch!

Another unusual finding was that consumers who patronized independent or non-dealer shops were 20% more satisfied than those going to the dealer. This agrees with the Car Kung Fu principle that dealer shops don't have much motivation to provide value because they get much of their business simply by virtue of being dealers — so watch out!

Finally — and this is worth remembering — customers who talked directly to the mechanic were one-third more satisfied than those who had to communicate through order writers. You know who they are — those guys in the clean white coats who do nothing but fill out those forms. If they were real mechanics, wouldn't they be in back fixing cars? The fact that they are not even allowed to work on your car tells you everything you want to know about order writers.

The bottom line on the survey comes from Martha Stewart, the executive director of the San Francisco-based organization. "Shop hard," she says, "and you'll find value."

In my experience, the independent is your best bet although a genuine service-station owner/operator is a good second choice. Be wary of the specialty shops. Don't patronize one without a pre-referral from an independent mechanic. Dealers suffer from a monstrous lack of incentive to provide top quality service at fair rates. Their ongoing new car sales provide them with an endless stream of service customers who really *can't* go anywhere else. Human nature being what it is, the prospect of picking up extra trade (yours!) just doesn't get their blood quite boiling anymore. Longtime drivers know that regular maintenance at the dealer, although predictable, can get just a little expensive. If you don't mind a little legwork, there may be better values to be had elsewhere.

And now the $64,000 question: *How do you find a good mechanic — and keep him?*

Well, if you have been paying attention, you have probably figured out by now that you really don't need simply one good mechanic; you may, in fact, need a handful of specialists, given the complexity of the modern motorcar.

Does this mean you should go out and assemble a cadre of pros in various fields on the off-chance that you may someday need one of them? Nope, not at all.

The Car Kung Fu method I like best is to find one independent shop with the following features:

- You deal directly with the owner. Even if the owner doesn't actually work on your car, you deal with him each and every time you come in.

- The owner does not act like the dealer does: treating customers like three-year-olds, feeding them coffee and claptrap, all the while keeping them from their cars and the real reason they came in. The owner will make an effort to get to know you and your car. And, if need be, will take you into the back room to show you what is going on.

- The owner understands the importance of refresher courses. He attends them himself and makes sure his top wrench-turners go also.

- The shop has a wonderful understanding of its limitations. It will tell you precisely the work it will not do, and, if you ask, recommend a shop that will. (Limitations usually will include such things as transmission work, engine rebuilding and especially complex electrical or diagnostic work.)

- The shop will, more often that not, be in a slightly out-of-the-way location. Chances are it will also have been there for a number of years. Being in an obscure location means that shop is not at the mercy of a crazed landlord who is forever raising the rent and forcing it to overcharge to stay in business. A shop that can generate volume in a side-street location probably has lots of word-of-mouth working for it.

- The shop will communicate that almost every major repair has options attached to it, and will explain these options as things progress. "We can get you a used part. Do you want one? Here is why we think you should get a new part...." While it is true that this process seems to waste the time of the shop, and seems to result in lower profits if the cheaper options are accepted, it will result in a happier customer and a lower likelihood of a misunderstanding later on.

OK, now you are salivating. How do you find such a shop? How you let the owner know that you want to be a good, loyal and steady customer? How do you get the best deal?

Finding the shop is not easy. You have to ask around. You have to ask people like police officers, taxi drivers, and fleet owners where they go. Or you can call your insurance company and ask it to recommend the shop it uses for investigatory work. (Hint: All car insurance companies investigate major claims before paying off. Usually they farm out this work to top-notch shops, shops they know will find out the real cause of the problem that gave rise to the claim. Getting the name of a shop from an insurance company will save you a lot of time!)

Once you find the shop, you have to check it out yourself. Eyeball it a little. You can even try the so-called broom test. Find out where the broom is supposed to be, and see if it is there. (The guy who dreamed this up really did have his synapses in the right firing order: he was trying to make the point that a shop that can't even manage itself, can't manage someone else's car!) If everything looks OK, the next step is to determine what equipment the shop has. Equipment is a good way to determine not only what a shop can actually do, but what a shop thinks it can do. Look for:

- An engine scope with computer interface that "interrogates" the computers on late model cars. Attached to the scope should also be a probe that fits in the exhaust pipe and tells the test equipment how well the engine is burning its fuel. Anyone who tells you that modern cars can be worked on without this $10,000 toy is spinning your air cleaner, friend.

- A dynamic (spinning) tire balancer. This will determine whether or not the shop is competent to do even a simple tire change. The cheaper bubble (static) balancers will not cut the mustard.

- A headlight alignment device. This will determine whether or not the shop is competent to attempt even to change a headlamp. Of course, you can change a lamp with only a screwdriver. Given the strength of today's beams, however, it is likely that the new bulb will blind an oncoming driver unless properly aligned. And that would make you, the owner, criminally liable for the consequences.

- A 4-wheel alignment bay (not to be confused with the older, cheaper 2-wheel systems.) This will determine whether or not the shop can either check your suspension or do any repair work to it. (All major suspension repair requires a 4-wheel alignment afterwards. Four-wheel alignment machines are not only costly, but — I promise I am not making this up — they, themselves, require an alignment once a month by a technician sent by the manufacturer.) If the shop says it subcontracts to another shop that has this equipment, the answer is acceptable.

How do you let the owner know you want to be a steady customer — and get the "perks" that come with being such a customer, including faster than usual service, quick help in case of an emergency, and, generally, extra attention to making sure you're happy? Simple: Tell him to his face. That's all there is to it.

How do you get the best deal? Pay attention to this: if you are dealing with a skilled, competent shop that is treating you fairly, that gets the job done right the first time (usually), that does not do work that does not have to be done, and that stands behind the work that is done, then you are already getting a better deal than 50% of all motorists out there. In our "time is money" world, simply botching the job the first time — a common problem because of the difficulty of diagnosing modern cars — puts the customer behind the eight-ball, regardless of whether the work on the first job is credited toward the second. (And often it is not. Often you are told that the earlier work "had to be done anyway.") Don't go looking for the 50%-off specials. Getting the right work done at the right price — no more, no less — is the biggest bargain in town.

We have talked a bit about mechanics — for mechanical repairs — but what about body shops for the cosmetic stuff?

First, body shops are a pain. I don't mean to tar the whole lot with the same brush but I have about had it with the body shop trade in general. First, in case you haven't noticed, there aren't that many of them around anymore. This is a direct result of the high cost of body shop equipment today, combined with the shortage of skilled body shop workers. It is also a direct cause of the total lack of customer service or respect at most outlets. Make no mistake: this is a "demand is greater than supply" business. As long as there are people who keep bumping into each other, and insurance companies standing by to approve the repair bill, the body shops can pretty much keep themselves busy all year round. They do not need — or perhaps even want — you or I to drop in requesting a non-insurance related repaint or rust touch-up. Nosirree, that sounds like work, and most of these shops are quite happy just swapping fenders and doors on cars that have been in minor collisions.

Also, most body shop operators equate good customer relations with putting a new ribbon in the adding machine. In case anyone from the industry is listening, it is annoying, not to say infuriating, to have someone poke around your vehicle, make chicken scratches on a pad, enter a bunch of numbers in a calculator, and then hand you a final total as if it were a gift from a higher power, carved in stone, etched on the heavens and unchangeable by man, woman or beast.

All right, enough screaming and yelling. In Car Kung Fu, we learn that we can get along with body shops by first learning how they work.

This may come as a surprise to you, but not all body shops do body work. In fact, most don't even like body work. First let me define my terms. Body work in this day and age has come to mean the specific process of prepping and painting body panels such as fenders, hoods and doors. If, for example, your car gets into a small fender bender, before the car can be repainted, the underlying metal must be reshaped and recontoured. The dents are filled in with putty, then sanded down. Then when everything is just right, the paint is mixed to match the old colour as closely as possible, and the panel is repainted. That's body work, and that's what most body shops do today.

BUT THE INSURANCE WAS SUPPOSED TO FIX IT

If you ask a lawyer to explain what insurance is, she will tell you that insurance is a financial instrument to compensate victims for damage and, where possible, put them back in the situation they were in prior to the loss. In the particular case of car insurance, the car you get back from the shop after your claim has been processed is supposed to be at least as good as it was before the accident. This is not often true, however. The rapid acceleration in car technology has confused the body shops even more than the mechanics. And the insurance adjusters — people who get paid, literally, to out-guess the body shops — are treading water also. Many accident-damaged cars today are written off, although they should not be. Worse, many cars are not written off when they should be — instead, an attempt is made to fix them. The one who suffers most from this second transgression is, of course, the owner who faithfully pays insurance premiums believing they offer protection in case of a loss.

If you are in a collision of any kind, do not assume the insurance adjusters know what they are doing, and do not automatically select a repair shop merely because the insurance company recommended it. Ask questions. Get a second opinion. Get a third opinion. If need be, get a lawyer. Demand your right to an "as-good-as" vehicle. Believe it or not, the basic principles of insurance haven't changed over the years. The willingness of the insurers to meet those obligations may have, however.

There was a time when body work meant something else. It meant that parts of the body were broken, bent or rusted, and had to be completely replaced. It meant the process of cutting out the bad parts of the body, with a blowtorch, and then taking virgin metal and building a piece to weld back in to make everything whole again. This process of cutting and welding is the kind of repair you might expect to make when a car is being treated for serious rust, or when a collision has damaged a portion of the metal so badly there is no other solution. In the real world, many body shops not only don't like doing these sort of repairs, they don't even know how to do them. The reason for this is that the skill of cutting and welding is much greater than simply shaping and painting. It is extremely labour intensive and one small mistake can spoil the whole job. If you are in the market for body work, make sure you understand the difference between the two types I have just described. If you want the sand and paint type, no problem. Any well located shop can help you out. If, however, your car needs the cut-and-weld type of work, be on your guard. You cannot trust this work to just any shop, even if the shop is willing to try it. You must do some homework first, asking around the garage circuit until you can get a line on someone who has the skill to do the job right.

Any other tricks about body shops?

Yep: Some shops do mainly collision work (insurance-related collision work, that is) and some don't. The ones that don't are more likely to relate to you, the customer, as a person than as a number. These are the shops that depend on word-of-mouth for their trade. To find them, you make word-of-mouth work for you. Ask around for recommendations. As in the case of mechanics, start with your insurance agent or bank manager. Then make a point of asking anyone who spends a lot of time in a car: police officers, sales representatives, taxi drivers, etc. A good Car Kung Fu tip is to locate a smallish used-car seller who seems to have presentable, quality stock — and ask *him* for the name of his body shop. All used-car sellers need a good body shop the way tires need air. The information is there for the asking!

A MECHANIC'S DIARY: A TYPICAL DAY IN THE LIFE OF A BUSY SHOP (BASED ON NOTES TAKEN BY THE SHOP OWNER)

A 1985 Ford Thunderbird with throttle body injection was waiting in the bay. The owner complained of stalling. The car was hooked to a scope and the ignition checked. Everything looked good. In fact, the ignition had been serviced quite recently and the plugs looked like they had seen less than 10,000 km of driving. Ford used an EEC IV in 1985 so we interrogated the unit electronically to see if any trouble codes might show up. We quickly turned up an intermittent "Code 23" which indicated the throttle position sensor was in trouble. We pulled the sensor and bench-tested it but, off the car, it checked out OK. This one was turning out to be a puzzler! Then we got lucky. While we were leaning over the engine to hook up our test instruments, we accidentally brushed against the main wiring harness and the engine stalled. Closer investigation showed that, on this model, the main harness was routed right past the EGR valve. The additional heat from the valve had turned the wiring to a sorry state. We replaced the entire harness and, once again, this Ford was ready to hit the road.

An '85 Nissan 300ZX, fresh from the body shop, was showing some very unusual symptoms. The in-dash security light was flashing continuously, an indication that the vehicle thought someone was constantly trying to break into it. We looked around for the culprit but, as near as we could see, all the doors were closed and everything was fine. And, even stranger, the air conditioner when activated, would only run in one setting: max. Very odd! Our first clue turned up while running through the standard diagnostic procedures Nissan publishes for the security system. The eighth step in the trouble-shooting schematic involved verifying the trigger at the front hood to check that it was correctly signalling the opening and closing of the hood assembly. We looked and looked but we couldn't find any trigger there at all! Then we remembered that the car had just come from a body shop. Sure enough, Nissan also parks an ambient temperature sensor under the front fender to help the climate control system figure out what it should be doing. The body technician who had worked on this car no doubt fell victim to the "spare parts" syndrome — i.e., he decided whatever parts he had left over after his work probably didn't need to be there in the first place.

Because of these two missing sensors, the vehicle was thoroughly convinced that it was in the process of being stolen during a heat wave. Hence, the security light and the max air conditioning!

An '83 Toyota Pickup was rolled into the shop with the ECM (electronic control module) completely blown — along with every other 12-volt electrical device the car had! That meant over $2,000 for a new ECM, along with assorted lights, buzzers and gauges. But first we had to find the problem so the condition wouldn't repeat itself. A visual inspection quickly turned up a corroded connection at the main junction block where the engine wiring harness meets the body connectors. This effectively cut the battery off from the charging system but didn't, by itself, explain the overload condition. Then we realized that this model used a separate voltage regulator — an unusual design by today's standards. Because of the position of the break, the voltage regulator ended up sensing low battery output — an understatement, considering the battery wasn't even connected — and tried to compensate by running about 20 volts through the system. The result was an overload for the electrical system. And for the owner's pocketbook.

By far our strangest case in years involved an '81 Colt front-drive with a fully electronic cooling fan. The owner complained that the alternator was acting strange. In order to get it to work she had to take the vehicle over 100 km/h. Only then did the dash warning light go out, and the alternator function normally (until the car was next turned off and restarted). The next trip, she would have to take it up to 100 km/h and start all over again!

We were expecting this one to be just a little hairy but even those expectations were exceeded when we found that the fuse to the alternator had blown out completely. Fine, except for one thing. Why did the alternator work only at high speeds? In fact, why did it work at all with the fuse gone? Where was it getting its power from? The "case of the haunted alternator" soon attracted every mechanic in the shop into the pit. We were getting nowhere until someone noticed that the electronic cooling fan seemed to be running all the time instead of cycling itself on and off. Hmm. A little more investigation revealed that the fan circuit had, sometime in the recent past, blown. Whoever fixed the problem had obviously been in a hurry. Such a hurry that they wired the fan directly to the main ignition feed, figuring that having a fan that was on all the time was preferable to a fan that was off all the time. (Getting it fixed properly would have been the best option, had anyone bothered!) The extra load on the circuit had quickly overloaded the charging system and then the alternator fuse had blown, leaving the car seemingly without an alternator. I say "seemingly" because our detective work didn't stop there.

At high speeds, we found, the "windmilling" of the fan blades through the natural air travel of highway driving had a peculiar effect on the tiny little DC motor that drove the fan itself. It made it act like a miniature generator! Since the fan circuit had been wired into the ignition feed, albeit foolishly, it provided a slight current , just enough to excite the alternator and wake it up. That's why the car had current from the time it reached highway speeds until the time it shut off. The owner, by the way, was surprised when she got a bill that included fixing the fan. Especially since she didn't even know it was broken!

6

The ABCs Of Car Mechanics

Hang on a sec. I know I promised you that Car Kung Fu is a theoretical course: no hands-on, no dirt under the fingernails.

Well, that doesn't mean you don't need at least a basic understanding of how the car works. Understanding a little can, I assure you, save you a lot.

Before we look at maintenance basics, let's spend a moment or so on the basic systems of the car.

ENGINE (INCLUDING VALVES AND RINGS)

Note: This section contains material which might negatively influence small children. Parental guidance is recommended.

Take an egg box and scissors. From the closed box cut out one egg-shaped section. Make sure you cut so the top and bottom come out together. (You could also perform all the exercises below with an empty egg-shaped pantyhose container.) Delicately open up the tiny container in front of you. Now drop a copper penny carefully into the bottom of the container and cover it with a thimbleful of gunpowder. (If you are out of gunpowder, that's OK. Just pretend.)

Close the two halves of the container and set it gently on the kitchen table. Get out a tube of instant glue and seal the egg so no one will ever open it up again. Now poke a tiny hole in the side of the egg with a sharp pointy instrument. (An icepick is best, but if you don't have an icepick, you can use a sharp pencil. If you don't have a sharp pencil, go back to pretending.)

Now put a short piece of construction-grade fast-burning fuse into the hole you made and light it up. (If you don't have a fuse, use ... well, heck, I think you get the idea by now!)

In a moment or two, if you have followed all the directions faithfully, you can expect a small explosion, forcing the copper penny down through the bottom of the egg and embedding it securely in your linoleum floor.

Congratulations! You have just made a tiny scale model of the workings of the modern engine.

Now consider how your model would work with these small changes:

- Each little egg (just like the one you made) is a cylinder. An eight-cylinder engine has eight of them.

- Modern engines don't use gunpowder. They use a carefully measured mix of air and gasoline. The air comes in through the air cleaner. And the gas comes from the gas tank where, presumably, you pumped it in, in the first place.

- Modern engines don't have fuses sticking out of each cylinder. Instead they have something even better. A spark plug. Each cylinder has its own plug embedded nose down inside so that the spark can ignite the air-fuel mixture. (The other half of the plug sticks out of the cylinder and has an ignition wire attached. On virtually any car, you can simply pop open the hood, trace the path of the ignition wires to the embedded plug, and see exactly where your cylinders are located.)

- No copper pennies either. Instead there are pistons inside each cylinder and the pistons are attached to a crankshaft. Modern engines are designed so that the explosions which take place many times a minute do not blow the pistons through the side of the car as in our demo — although, I swear to you, this does actually happen every now and then. Instead, the crankshaft absorbs the force of the ongoing explosions and turns the flywheel. The flywheel turns the transmission, the transmission turns the driveshaft, the driveshaft turns the wheels, and the wheels make the tires move. I think you are getting the idea now.

- The modern engine is slightly more complex. Getting the air-fuel mixture to the cylinders is tricky because at the exact time of the explosion — just as in your scale model — the cylinders have to be sealed tight to do the most good. (Remember the glue?) This is accomplished by small doors called valves in the top of each cylinder. The intake valve opens just before firing to let in the air-fuel mixture, and the exhaust valve opens just after firing to let the burnt gases out (they are sent to the exhaust pipe). The whole in-explode-out cycle, taking place rapidly in many cylinders at the same time, is what creates the illusion the engine is running "smoothly."

- Getting the spark to the spark plug at exactly the right time, not a second too soon or too late, is also pretty important. This used to be handled by a device called a distributor which looked like an upside down pencil holder, and was just about as attractive. Nowadays, many distributors have been replaced with sensors and transistors. This particular function is now much more complicated and, some would say, not much more efficient.

- Rings are fitted around the pistons. Rings are, strangely, the hardest part of the process to explain without having a real engine in front of you. Imagine putting a ring around your finger about half-way down and then sticking your finger into a cigar tube. The finger is the moving piston, the cigar tube the cylinder, and the ring is the ring. In fact, the rings (there are more than one) act as a fence does between properties. On the upper side of this particular fence is the air-fuel mixture we have been talking about. And on the bottom is your engine oil under extreme pressure as it lubricates the crankshaft and other moving parts. This is no ordinary fence either: it moves up and down with the moving piston — or, if you prefer, moving finger. As long as the fence keeps things apart, there is no problem. However, once the fence weakens, the high-pressure oil rushes past to join the air-fuel mixture, gets burned with the mixture, and sends blue oily smoke out the tailpipe. Hence the expressions "oil burner" and "bad rings."

FUEL SYSTEM

The carburetor, now virtually extinct, was just a mix-valve in which air from the air cleaner and gas were mixed in the right proportions. The mixture was then delivered or "mailed" to the individual cylinders along the intake manifold, an interconnected series of highways that dead-end at the intake valve of each cylinder. On the more modern cars, the intake runners deliver only air, and the raw gas is delivered by fuel injectors that are embedded in the cylinders (just like the spark plugs). Modern fuel systems are designed to be maintenance-free, as long as the consumer does three things: changes the air cleaner regularly; changes the gas filter regularly; and uses only gasoline certified by the manufacturer not to foul its injectors. Since nobody does all three of these things, modern fuel systems tend to be very troublesome over the long term.

IGNITION SYSTEM

Remember points and condensors? If so, your age is showing. Almost all systems since the eighties use electrical triggers, instead of mechanical ones, to prod the ignition voltage coil into sending sparks to the spark plug at the perfect moment. Ignition systems used to be the most fragile part of the car, now they are among the toughest. Anyone who tries to get more than three or four years off one set of ignition components — plugs, wires, distributor cap, distributor rotor — is, nonetheless, asking for grief.

CHARGING SYSTEM

Your battery "works" only when you start the car. Thereafter, it "rests" and receives current from the charging system which revives it until you shut the engine off. To get the most life out of the battery, the charging system must deliver the right voltage range for your battery, no more and no less. If it varies, battery life is diminished. Most batteries in most climates will hang in there for about four years. The alternator—the component most responsible for keeping the battery charge—will usually last six to ten years and then die a sudden, horrible death.

EXHAUST SYSTEM

This system is just a bunch of pipes and tubes that keep those deadly exhaust gases from asphyxiating you, the driver, and instead dump them into the area just behind the car where they can mix into the air and hurt everybody you've left behind. Most of these components need replacement every three or four years. (The closer to the back of the car a part is, the faster it will wear.) Inside this system is also the nefarious converter, a $300 box full of strange-sounding chemicals that filter the exhaust gas as it goes through. The converter should last about ten years, all things being equal. (Which, of course, they never are.)

TRANSMISSION OR GEARBOX

The problem facing this component is how to get the movement of the flywheel translated into something that will make the driveshaft, and the wheels, turn. To make things even more interesting, the force of the engine should be geared to make most efficient use of its power in different situations. (The ten-speed gears on a bike have a similar function. Professional racers know that, with constant pumping, it is the gears that give them the edge in key situations.) All this is accomplished by one of two ways: either a clutch and gearbox (the "manual") or a monstrous electronic and/or hydraulic unit which selects the proper gear for you (the illustrious "automatic"). The manual gearbox is a surprisingly simple (and durable) item. The automatic, on the other hand, usually has more passageways, valves, tunnels and other paraphernalia than a ride at Disneyland.

And the most recent trend is even more ominous. A whole generation of mechanical beasties called ECTs (electronically controlled transmissions) are being vended with the premise that smart, reliable little transistors, switches and diodes are better than dumb, stupid hydraulic valves and pumps. Is this true? The answer, as with most things automotive, is yes and no. When an ECT needs help, it *really* needs help. As early as 1989, an interesting article in *Motor Magazine* (the mechanic's bible) suggested that problems in ECT can easily mimic a defective or ill-tuned engine. The thrust of the article was that, after you have spent $5,000 trying to fix the engine of the customer's car with no obvious improvement, you may find that the problem lies in the ECT.

SUSPENSION (AND STEERING)

Now the car is moving, you really want something between you and the road to absorb all those dips and potholes. Springs, struts and shocks perform this function. While you turn the wheel from the comfort of the driver's seat, the steering mechanism has to perform a complex number of functions at more or less the same time:

- steer the car;
- keep the wheels more or less in correct geometry with the road surface, so the tires last for months, not merely hours;
- provide a certain degree of feedback, so the driver knows what is going on;
- magnify the force of the driver so even a 45-kilogram weakling can drive a two-tonne hunk of iron.

The type of suspension you have depends largely on the model year. Pre-eighties rear-drive cars had rough and tough suspensions, generally, a combination of springs and shocks. The shocks were good for about five years, and the springs for about ten. Neither repair was particularly expensive. Front-drive cars brought in the strut assembly, something I for one could have lived without. (These units performed the same essential function as shocks but didn't last as long. And they cost about five times as much.) Buried inside the steering system are all sorts of oddball parts to make a mechanic's life more interesting. Generally speaking, the simpler the system, the longer it lasts. For example, old-fashioned recirculating-ball steering will last almost forever. You can't say the same about the power-assist rack-and-pinion units that everyone seems to like nowadays. For the nineties, computer-controlled suspensions should make a suspension repair about as expensive as a new engine. Thanks, guys.

COOLING/HEATING SYSTEM

People often mix up the heating and air conditioning systems. And for good reason. The heater in your car merely forces into the car's interior air that has picked up the heat from the engine's internal coolant mixture, which is already *hot* as a result of the normal engine activity. (Why coolant? The liquid mix that circulates through the system picks up heat from the engine and carries it to the radiator. There, air from the fan cools the liquid. It is then recycled back to the engine, and so it continues. Therefore, coolant really does keep the engine cool. Without it, the engine could easily melt.)

Air conditioning, if you have it, really is a cooling system! If present, it is an entirely separate, and relatively unreliable, sub-system that uses a refrigerant to keep things cool. It is sufficiently complex to deserve a book all its own.

The base heating/cooling system, meanwhile, is not as simple as it looks. Interestingly, drivers will often allow their cars to reach near melt-down in spite of all the warning they will get from dashboard lights. (It is, in fact, technically impossible to abuse the engine to the point of true melt-down, since the pistons will expand inside their cylinders and the engine will "seize" or stop running.)

BRAKING SYSTEM

This hydraulic system has not changed too much over the years. Front discs work on the principle of the grabbing hand. A pincer-like apparatus grasps the discs which, themselves, are all-metal wheels hidden just behind the front tires. The rear drums, if present, work differently. An expanding set of shoes rubs against the inside of a rotating drum and so forces the car to slow down.

Downsizing of brake parts to save weight has meant they need servicing a lot more often than they used to. Also, the abandonment of asbestos in brake parts (it's a killer) has meant the use of replacement materials which, quite simply, don't last as long or do as good a job. The only other major change for the nineties is anti-lock braking (ABS), a system which, in theory, stops the car faster under all conditions. (It doesn't work better under *all* circumstances, but let's not be picky. It's still a good idea.) ABS , like electronic transmissions, is new. There is not enough data to extrapolate into the year 2000. My guess, however, is that the cost of fixing your ABS if it is seriously on the fritz will be somewhere between that of a new set of tires and a trip to Europe.

COMPUTERS

Almost all cars since 1985 include a computer. And if you think the computer in your home or office is more complex than the one under your hood, then you are wrong. Some cars have as many as three main processors getting input from 20-30 sensors. That's a lot of information to process, and it leaves room for a lot of things to go wrong. It would be dandy if the computers and the sensors themselves never failed. If that were true, then the only things left to wear out would be the mechanical bits and pieces that the sensors were, ah, sensing. That arrangement would appeal even to me although, as a rule, I welcome computers in cars as much as screen doors in submarines. Unfortunately, this is not the case. Not only do the mechanical bits and pieces wear out (as we might expect) but the sensors and the main processors will also fail over time. (Congratulations! — I think that, together, between the two of us, we have just figured out why, although automobile repair volume is down, unit repair costs are up!)

All you really have to know about computers is that it is important to deal with a mechanic who can talk to the computer in your car and ask it what is really going on inside its pretty little head.

Aside from prayer, there is no other maintenance to speak of.

WOW!

As if computers in cars were not a sufficiently complex phenomenon all by themselves, I should mention that emission laws play a part in this drama also. Specifically, the makers use the precision of computers to monitor emissions, as well as to run the car and increase fuel economy. Now the plot thickens even more. Since emissions are regulated by tough federal laws which make manufacturers responsible for the car's pollutants during the first few years of its life, car companies are quite sensitive to the prospect of anyone trying to tamper with or adjust their precious computers in any way. And that, dear reader, brings me to my favourite story culled from 20 years of research as a car journalist.

According to reliable sources, a computer engineer had purchased a mid-eighties BMW and was thoroughly unhappy with the performance of the car (a not-uncommon situation for BMW owners of that era). He asked BMW for the specs on the computer chip which controlled such useful things as spark timing, fuel delivery, etc. — only to be stonewalled by the recalcitrant manufacturer. This consumer, however, did not take "no" for an answer. He installed about $50,000 worth of test equipment on his dashboard so he could "monitor" the computer's handling of his engine and learn, by watching it, how it had been originally programmed. Once he "broke the code," he reprogrammed the chip and finally got the performance he'd craved from his own car!

EMISSION SYSTEM

Trust me — you don't really want to know about all the strange things on your engine that are there for no other purpose than to keep the emissions where they should be. Keep the following in mind, however: an on-the-fritz emission control device can disable your car as surely as a bad engine or transmission can. The diagnostic time needed to pinpoint troubles in these systems is simply awesome. Not surprisingly, there is no standardization from maker to maker, or even model to model. The only good news is that the warranty on these parts can often exceed the warranty on the car itself by four or five years, and subsequent owners are covered. (At least, all this works in theory. In 1989, Chrysler was heavily fined by the US Government for making a customer pay for emission-related repairs!)

UNIBODY CONSTRUCTION

These days you can't discuss cars for more than a few minutes without someone pointing out that they don't build 'em like they used to — literally! The point is well taken: almost all the cars on the road today are "unibody" construction, with the exception of a handful of older "body-on-frame" designs. This is in sharp contrast to, for example, the situation during the sixties or early seventies when things were quite reversed: most cars were body on frame, with only a handful of unibody models.

The difference? What differentiates a piece of railroad track from an eggshell? That's what separates these two types of construction also.

Body-on-frame construction bolted bits and pieces of the body to a solid extra-thick metal frame underneath. The frame was tough and strong with the approximate dimensions of railroad ties. Whatever happened to the body panels, things were still 100% salvageable as long as the frame was strong and intact.

Unibody imitates nature's own construction marvel: the eggshell. There is no frame, but every piece is meshed with every other piece so well that incredible strength is achieved. (Did you ever try to break an egg in one hand while applying equal pressure on the sides? You can't.)

As you might guess at this stage in your study of Car Kung Fu, the unibody design makes a lot of sense until something gets busted or goes wrong. Then, like everything else on the new cars, it is both expensive and complicated to fix. (Unibody equipment plus a trained operator is an absolute must.)

Any mistake made in fixing a unibody car can mean trouble down the road. Take just one example. When rust ate a large hole in the floor of my little Mazda GLC, on the driver's side, I had the repair done by a shop that claimed to be experienced in unibody. They patched the hole with a large sheet of metal which, they told me, left the floor in even better condition than when new.

Except for one thing: Every time I take a corner or hit a bump, I can hear that patch flex and groan. The noise is an excellent reminder how, in a unibody design, even parts that seem isolated — such as the floor area under the driver's feet — are structurally inter-related to every other piece of the body.

7

Maintenance You Can Live With

A TRUE STORY

She looked like the proverbial little old lady from Pasadena. Grey hair, silver spectacles, sensible shoes. Everything fit except for the car she was driving: a late-model top-of-the-line Japanese sports car with all the trimmings. She seemed nervous waiting in line at the service desk. The technician who spoke to her was also ill at ease. What was the problem? "I have had this car four years and there are over 50,000 km on it," she admitted. "Aside from oil changes, I have done absolutely nothing to it. Everything is original. Original spark plugs. Original antifreeze. Original everything. The car runs fine. But I am getting a little worried about my good luck. What do you think?"

Not only is this story true — the mechanic who told it to me is still shaking his head — but it is typical. If you are driving a late-model car, chances are that you, too, are attending to your car poorly. According to a recent series of studies done by independent analysts, the frequency of car service, over-all, is way down. (There are more cars on the road each year, however, so this tends to mask the visibility of this peculiar trend.) But the cost per repair is way up!. People drive their

135

vehicles until something breaks, or the car won't start. Then, when they are hit with a $700-$1,400 repair bill, they don't complain because, deep in their hearts, they feel they are paying for the sin of neglect. And, of course, they are. Only one problem, folks: contrition is not what Car Kung Fu is all about! Savings, however, is.

Let's examine the basic maintenance myths — and then scrape them, whittle them away, and, with luck, separate fact from fiction in the process.

TUNE–UPS

In your grandparents' day, the ignition and fuel systems of North America's motorcars were effective but not particularly durable. Spark plugs needed cleaning and regapping about every 3,000 km, and replacement at 9,000 km. The low-tech (and inexpensive) spark plug wires — the wires that carry ignition to each cylinder — lasted about one rough winter before they started to give trouble. Points and condensor, the dynamic duo that triggered each individual ignition spark, were good for 12,000 km — maybe. (A point file, a 50-cent tool to clean the points, was a common component of a mechanic's toolbox. Today, they're to be found only in museums.)

The very word "tune-up" was coined to describe servicing the ignition — and very little else. Such tune-ups, however frequent, were not that expensive. The distributor rotor and cap, together, cost only a few dollars and they were usually replaced at the same time as the points and plugs. If the ignition voltage coil showed any arcing or cracking, it too was inexpensively replaced in the process. And let's not forget that old mechanical carburetor. This amazing contraption, which seemingly had more moving parts than today's washing machines, inevitably needed constant loving and pampering, plus dozens of tiny little adjustments, in order to keep performance and fuel consumption within proper limits — and by that we're talking approximately 15 litres/100 km!

Now let's look at today's chariots. A high-voltage electronically triggered (pointless) ignition, combined with premium lead-free gasoline, means that your spark plugs and ignition system should perform quite reliably, without fuss, for up to 40,000 km between servicings (although some manufacturers may recommend servicing before that). The wires, coil, cap and rotor should last almost as long as the plugs. (That's assuming your car has a separate distributor in the first place. Many cars today don't.) As for the fuel system, don't even *think* of trying to adjust it unless you have a Ph.D. in electronics and a warehouseful of test equipment.

Note also that when a new car leaves the factory, certain specifications in the electrical and fuel systems are set precisely. The reason for this precision is that government emission laws have to be met and only specific, calibrated settings will do so. As the car wears over normal use, these settings change slightly all by themselves. Furthermore, if the car is brought to a mechanic for any service whatsoever, he may alter these settings even more to make the car run better. Therefore — and this is the important part — after a few years the car is really no longer running at the specifications it was when it left the factory.

So far, so good. Now, you bring the car in for a tune-up. Here's what happens. In theory, the mechanic doing the tune-up on today's modern car should check the settings the car is currently performing at, and, if everyone is happy with the car's performance, try to keep those settings through the tune-up. But very few do that. Instead, the vast majority will simply replace basic ignitions parts like plugs and wires. That's where their profit is — new parts. Next they will simply reset everything to those original factory specifications. To most shops today that's all a tune-up is: replace and reset.

But is this replace and reset procedure really needed? And, if so, when? According to experts, all you really need to keep chugging along during most of your car's useful life is a good quality fuel, replacement gas filters as needed and, occasionally, a bottle of fuel injector cleaner. Modern ignition parts should not be replaced unless they are defective or severely worn. Modern fuel systems, as explained, are totally non-adjustable. And the seasonal tune-up has veritably gone the way of the dodo bird.

Except for one small problem. A lot of mechanics out there have managed to develop a strong sentimental attachment to that old-style tune-up — an attachment that might have more to do with finances than feelings. The numbers tell the real story: these days an ignition tune-up (new plugs, silicone wires, cap and rotor) can easily run well over $150. And that's assuming the car ran well when it first rolled in! The fact that these new bits and pieces may not absolutely be needed often tends to be overlooked — particularly if the owner gives the mechanic a "blank cheque" to work with.

So what's the answer? First, eliminate the word "tune-up" from your vocabulary. If your preferred shop likes the word, eliminate the shop also. If your car's driveability changes for any reason, or the check engine light comes on and stays on, then go ahead and have things looked at. Other than that, have your ignition system serviced no earlier than every 30,000 km and no later than every 45,000 km. At this juncture you should have the plugs, cap and wires changed, the ignition should be "scoped," and the exhaust gas should be checked to make sure the emissions are within the correct tolerances.

And if anyone, should try to get you to have a tune-up for no other reason than that the seasons have changed, strike that person off your Christmas list. He or she is wasting your time, and your money.

A LIQUID LUNCH FOR YOUR CAR — PLUS OTHER TIPS FROM A PRO

One top mechanic shared with me a procedure he uses with his customers' modern cars: prior to doing any ignition or carburetor work, he will add a can of crankcase flush to the engine and let it idle for a while. Then he will change the oil. Next he will add a can of upper cylinder cleaner to the air intake (or carb) and let it run through. Only at that point will he service the ignition. His thinking — verified by successful results in his shop — is that modern computerized engines are sensitive to any junk or foreign matter in the individual cylinders, which might clog the valves or rings. By following this procedure before he plays with the electronics, he is making sure the engine is best prepared to make use of the new plugs and other ignition parts he will be installing. (He showed me examples of this method in action in his shop. Even engines with poor compression — an indication that the valves and rings were seating poorly — would pop back to life after this technique.)

That same tune-up expert also makes extra points with his clientele by actually servicing the distributor, as opposed to merely changing its cap and rotor. The distributor is physically removed from the car and the rust coating that inevitably collects on the balance weights is removed by hand. The entire mechanism is thoroughly lubed with an oilcan, and the whole part is then bench-tested before reinstallation.

Finally, no tune-up leaves his shop until all vacuum devices are checked by hand with a portable vacuum pump. Vacuum devices are not complex: many valves throughout the emission system open or close only when engine vacuum is directed their way. The system is so simple that many mechanics take it for granted — and they shouldn't. A bad vacuum diaphragm will not only negatively affect the device it's hooked to. It will also produce lower overall engine performance because of the "lean burn" condition caused by leaking outside air into the cylinders and throwing off the preset air-fuel ratios. Checking these devices for leaks takes little time, and virtually ensures that the servicing will yield the right results.

OIL CHANGES

If I said that oil isn't really oil, you might think that I had flipped a gasket. But it isn't. At least, it's not oil in the sense that all it does is lubricate. Oil is actually a complex chemical soup of which lubricating additives are just a small component. Oil also controls the pH of your engine, works to prevent foaming, works to prevent deposits from forming on engine parts, works to protect critical parts from feeling extreme pressure, plus cleans and scrubs as it circulates.

Wait, there's more! A huge component of oil is a polymer formula that allows oil to have what I call "chameleon" properties; i.e., it permits the oil to flow at the rate your engine needs, relative to its operating temperature.

Let's stop for a moment and review the "oil conundrum." The heavier the weight of the oil (i.e., the thicker it is), the better it protects, especially during the hot operating conditions produced by an engine that has been running for a while. Just one tiny problem: thick oil will congeal like Jell-O during cold weather and, although it still protects well enough, it will fight the starter motor and keep the engine from firing. Unless you move to a tropical climate, that is.

The solution? Thin oil, of course. Thin oil will actually help the starter turn the engine over, even in cold weather. Especially in cold weather. Trouble is, once the engine fires up, there is no real protection left for the delicate moving parts, as the heat of the engine's operation dilutes and thins the oil even further.

That's the "oil conundrum." Thin oil — good starting but rotten protection. Thick oil — great protection but no cold-weather starting.

So what oil do you use if you *don't* live in Hawaii?

Until about 20 years ago, there was no solution. People were advised to pick the thickest weight of oil tolerable for their climate. In the manual that came with my brand-new 1971 VW, I was advised to do the following in winter: fill the crankcase with a thin oil so the car would start easily, then, before a long trip, change the oil to a heavier grade. After the car was at its destination, I was advised to switch back to a thin oil so the car would start reliably the next morning.

THE ABCs OF TSBs

There is now a brand new piece of electronic wizardry to look for. A computerized TSB database. TSB stands for Technical Service Bulletins. TSBs are published by the car companies whenever they find a problem that is common to one or more of the cars they sell. If you are thinking that a lot of models have problems in common, then you are one giant step ahead of me. In fact, hundreds of TSBs are published by each car company each month, adding up to thousands per car company per year. Now, wouldn't it be just peachy if *your* corner mechanic had access to all these TSBs so that, when *you* came rolling in with *your* problem, he could fix it even quicker? Of course it would be nice. But also impractical. To keep all the TSBs handy, your mechanic would practically have to run his own library. Or he could go out and purchase one of the new computerized TSB databases which allow access to tens of thousands of TSBs at the mere push of a button.

The solution to these problems was the multi-weight or multi-grade oil, the oil you and I take for granted when we go for an oil change and ask for 10-40 or 5-30. The lower number is the real weight of the oil, usually a thin weight so the engine will start easily and, once running, turn easily using the least amount of gas. The higher number is weight the oil will "imitate," thanks to its polymer additives, when the engine gets hot and needs extra protection.

Everything inside your engine is fine just as long as the additives keep switching the oil weight back and forth, invisibly, while you drive. Trouble is, the additives are the first part of the "oil soup" to wear out.

Let me rephrase that. The lubrication parts of your oil last a long time. But the polymer additives that constantly change the weights wear quickly. And invisibly. In other words, if you are using 10-40 oil in a hot summer climate, and you wait too long between changes, you are really using only 10-weight oil, period. And 10-weight oil will not protect your engine's innards too well in a hot clime!

The solution? Regular oil changes, at least every three months, for all drivers. Regardless of mileage. This is the same system taxi drivers use and they get spectacular wear from their machines. Regardless of what it may say in the manual, change the filter at the same time as the oil. It's not worth the risk!

AN OIL ADDITIVE THAT MAY WORK!

The only things we know for certain about off-the-shelf oil additives is that (a) the oil manufacturers hate them (claiming that, if the additive were any good, it would already be in their oil); and (b) the people who sell them drive more expensive cars than you or I do. You may draw your own conclusions from the above. Let me mention that, over the years, I have encountered one additive which I have grown rather attached to. It's called Tufoil, and it is available by mail and in certain stores. The additive has a Teflon base and claims to reduce friction and improve fuel economy and performance. Does it work? Maybe. In my own vehicles I have noticed easier starting in cold weather — of this I have no doubt. I have also seen some data collected at a cold-weather test centre in Northern Ontario, one that is normally utilized by the Canadian government to test its own cars. In the test, a series of VW Rabbit diesel engines were cranked over using only the starter motor. In the next round of testing, the very same engines were turned over under the same conditions with Tufoil added to the crankcase. The net result was about 10% higher r.p.m. (cranking rotations) with the additive. This is, by the way, the only test I've ever seen of a friction reducer which tries to eliminate variables such as driver action and fuel/ignition interference. I admit it: I'm impressed.

VALVES

I once did a story for a magazine in which I pointed out that, next to oil changes, valve adjustments were the single most important maintenance operation to be performed on modern cars. The editor was indignant: "You must be kidding," he said. "I have never heard of a valve adjustment and I have been driving for 40 years." Time to wake up and smell the coffee, pal. Because of North America's recent love affair with four- and six-cylinder engines, I estimate that more than 60% of all the cars on the road today require regular adjustments to the slack in the valve-train. (This procedure takes the average mechanic about an hour in labour and about $20 in parts.) Failure to do this will not make your engine fail absolutely, but it will make it fail earlier than it should. How early? Most engines should last about 150,000 to 175,000 km before the valves and rings start to cause problems. Without regular valve adjustments (and oil changes) you can cut this number in half. Why have you never heard of valve adjustments before? Because the operation is so labour-intensive, and the profit margin it offers is so low, that manufacturers and the service industry don't feel it's worth their while to educate the public about it. Besides, what's wrong with your engine conking out at 75,000 km anyway? Time to buy a new one!

How do you know if your particular vehicle needs a valve adjustment? Look in your owner's manual and see if "valve service," "valve lash" or "valve clearance" is listed at regular intervals — say every 25,000 km or so. If it is, you have just discovered an important maintenance item which you might not have been aware of. (If you have lost the manual, call the dealer or the maker.)

FILTERS

Ironically, filters have become smaller (and less efficient) in order to fit under the hood of today's smaller cars. Make sense to you? It sure doesn't to me: anyone who's ever used a coffee maker knows that smaller filters need changing more often. Anyway, your oil filter should be changed at every oil change, and the air and gasoline filters according to your owner's manual. This is very inexpensive insurance against trouble down the line.

THE RIGHT STUFF FOR YOUR GAS TANK

If your car has fuel injectors, you may be shocked to learn that not all gasolines are created equal. Some are more likely to clog injectors than others. See your owner's manual for the right advice, or phone your manufacturer's head office.

TIRES

Every year some company or other does a survey and concludes that over 30% of all motorists are driving around with seriously underinflated tires. These drivers are taking a safety risk they really don't have to take. Underinflation means a much greater likelihood of blowouts. Why are so many drivers taking these chances? I think the reason is that a lot of us don't know what the tire pressure should be or — I'm not kidding — can't figure out how to work the air pump at the gas station.

The correct tire pressure for your vehicle is given in at least two places: the owner's manual, and on a special sticker hidden away inside your car. The special sticker will usually be in the glove box lid or the trunk lid, or most likely, on the inside of the door jamb. To interpret the sticker correctly you may need to know in advance what size tires you have, because some cars specify different pressures for different tire sizes. The tire size is, of course, marked on your tire.

Now what about those gas station air pumps? The truth is that most don't work that well. Before choosing an air pump, you should first make sure that the gauge on the thing works. It's supposed to shut off automatically when the marked pressure is reached. Also check that the air chuck — that part you stick on your tire — is functioning properly.

To make sure that the gauge on the pump will shut off at the marked pressure, you will need to bring a spare hand-held gauge with you on your first fill-up, and check the main gauge against it. However — here's the good news— once you've checked it, you can then rely on the main gauge, that's the one on the pump, for all your subsequent tire check-ups.

Now what about that air chuck, the little metal part you stick on your tire? To make sure it works at all, jam your thumbnail into the indent that protrudes just slightly from the mouth of the chuck. Air should whoosh out for a moment. Also, keep in mind that a badly adjusted chuck will leak air out of your tire instead of filling it. So, if you fill your tires and end up with less air than you started with, you've found a bad air chuck. Either tell the station owner, or find a new station to get air at ... and then start all over.

If you fill regularly and still find your tires are low, you have a leak. What to do about it? A student of mine had a sports car with a tire that was always losing air. The car had cost him over $30,000, each of the tires was worth over $150, and now he was worried he would have to pay a mechanic another $50 to find the difficulty. He was frustrated, to say the least. I explained to him that slow leaks usually originate in one of three places. The first is the tread where a small nail or piece of glass can cause the problem. We examined the tire and found no evidence of puncture. If we had, I would have sent him to a mechanic, because punctures on a radial tire require a special repair process that must be done by a qualified person.

The next most common cause of slow leaks is poor sealing around the wheel rim. This particular cause is hard to track down: it may have originated from a bad installation when the tires were first mounted, or from a defective tire, from a defective wheel rim, or even from damaging the rim by sloppy parking.

To clear up these particular problems, you have to call in a specialist to stick the tire and wheel in a tub of water and see where the leak is coming from. If the leak is repairable, you will also have to have the tire and rim assembly remounted and rebalanced. At the worst, you will need a new tire or a new rim. I told my friend that if this was the cause of his problem he was out of luck and would have to see a pro.

However, there was one more possibility, the third most likely cause of a leaky tire. The valve may have gone bad. I unscrewed the valve cap on the bad tire to expose the valve. I next put a little saliva into the valve to check for escaping air. (Soap suds will work also, by the way.) Sure enough, within two seconds of my putting saliva into the valve, an air bubble forced its way out the valve. Bingo — the problem had been caused by a bad valve! The solution? We went to the auto shop and purchased a pack of new valves, at a cost of $1.99, and a small tool to change the valve, at a cost of $1.50. Using the tool, I unscrewed the old valve from the valve stem and screwed the new one in. We lost a lot of air in the process so I made sure we did this next to an air pump. The whole process took three minutes. Hey — who says car service is complex?

TURBOS

If you are driving a turbo-charged car right now, pay attention. Since mass production turbo-charging first came out in the late sixties, I have repeatedly emphasized two points. The first is that, while turbo-charging provides extra power, it also tends to turn your car into a gas guzzler. The second point is that a turbo engine is a complicated piece of machinery. And the more complex the car, the more likely things are to go wrong. Especially if you keep the car more than four or five years. If, after digesting this information, you go out and get a turbo anyway, congratulations on being a free thinker. Now, let's look at what your non-conformity might cost you.

A Car Kung Fu student owned a late '70s turbo-charged Buick. Engine power was down, blue smoke came out the tailpipe, and the car made strange sounds on acceleration. Diagnosis showed it needed a complete turbo replacement, due to wear. The owner loved her turbo and was more than willing to pay the bill. When the dealer finally provided her with the replacement turbo hardware, the owner had the foresight to get it checked by her own mechanic first. The mechanic reported that the stuff was junk and advised against installing it. Very well, said the dealer when the assembly was returned, we'll take the part back. But that was our last one. We are now completely out of stock on turbo replacement parts. It could be as long as six months before the manufacturer sends us any more.

"Ouch," said the owner who suddenly decided that having a turbo engine didn't really mean that much to her after all. She then went back to her own private mechanic and paid to convert the turbo-charged Buick engine into a regular non-turbo engine. The conversion was not cheap and took several weeks to complete. But the owner was now happy. Very happy. She no longer felt she was at the mercy of strange technology or unsympathetic dealers and parts people. She no longer felt that she was driving a car that was non-fixable. And, most of all, she did not miss the extra power of the turbo in day-to-day driving. Not at all. (In case you think I am being unfair to single out Buick, let me quickly add that I also have several dozen reports of turbo engines from other makers which are causing their owners nothing but headaches as they age.)

So, in the ten years I have been complaining about turbos, the bottom line really hasn't changed. My advice is: Stay away. And here's another Car Kung Fu tip: Don't be tempted by options or gadgets that can't be explained by one eight-year old to another in less than 90 seconds. This test has always worked for me!

ALIGNMENTS

> *To align or not to align, that is the question. Whether 'tis*
> *nobler (and more cost-effective) to align all four*
> *wheels, or merely two?*
> *Should one align, or merely make do?*
> *To align, to pay through the nose for something one can't*
> *feel or touch?*
> *Why should I bother? On my last car, alignments hardly*
> *mattered that much!*
> *Or perhaps I'll do nothing, but drive and drive. The tires*
> *may moan but my wallet will surely thrive!"*

True, Hamlet never asked these particular questions. But, if he drove a late-model car, Horatio, he might have. Honest.

What is "alignment" anyway? There is a certain preferred geometry in the way all four tires are positioned, relative to the car's chassis. If that geometry is respected, you can count on your vehicle to deliver maximum tire-tread life, as well as optimal handling and braking performance.

Ignore this preferred geometry, or allow a serious alignment problem to go undetected and/or uncorrected, and you are asking for extremely accelerated tread wear (often up to ten times the normal rate), as well bizarre or unpredictable handling and braking characteristics.

All cars need front alignments from time to time. Take that as gospel. But, do all cars need 4-wheel alignment?

Well, yes — and no.

The old Detroit body-on-frame hogs of the '60s with fixed (non-independent) rear suspensions had little, if any, allowance built in for monkeying with the rear wheels. Assuming the car had not been in a serious accident (which, incidentally, is the easiest way to turn any vehicle into a candidate for 4-wheel service), then the service technician's main concerns were simply to make sure that the rear suspension was not deteriorating in any way, and that the rear wheels were in line with the front.

The advent in the seventies of unibody cars with independent suspensions (all four wheels can move independently) opened up a Pandora's box of things that could go wrong with the rear tires. Not only did the rear of the vehicle have to be headed in the same direction as the front, but now the cars were coming from the factory with full alignment specifications (angles) for the rear wheels, much like the ones that came with the front pair.

And the even more recent popularity of 4-wheel-drive vehicles brought home the need for 4-wheel alignment machinery to an even greater extent. Although practical in certain situations, 4-wheel-drive power-trains have many more moving parts than 2-wheel-drive cars. These parts seem to get out of alignment even faster than their 2-wheel-drive counterparts. (Alignment of 4-wheel-drive machines requires not only a special 4-wheel alignment machine but also a lot of patience. Many calibrations have to be done by trial and error, using hand-installed shims to reach the right settings.)

Another irony is that many body shops of borderline competence — unable to afford the equipment to repair and test the new unibody cars fully — rely on 4-wheel alignment shops to catch errors that should have been fixed during the original repair, rather than to verify that the repair work was done correctly the first time. (One alignment shop owner I interviewed confessed that his biggest customer was the body shop across the street, always using his machine to see if they got the job right!)

Whether the alignment is 4-wheel or 2-wheel, it is important to choose a shop with a reputation for honesty and integrity. Since all alignment work requires that a thorough check be made of the suspension parts before the job is done, it is important that the technician not be overly enthusiastic — or larcenous — in his recommendation as to which parts need replacing.

One of my students had an itchy feeling about taking his favourite Volvo to a local dealership for an alignment, so he stopped first at an auto club inspection centre to have the front end inspected for worn parts. The verdict: The front end was in fine shape, no new parts needed. Once the car was on the rack in the dealer service bay, however, a different story emerged. Some $300 in parts were needed before the technician would even consider attempting an alignment. "Don't touch that car," said the student, and whisked his way back to the trusty inspection centre. There, yet another mechanic was summoned to poke and prod the front end, only to determine that, as before, the parts were all in fine shape.

What is there about the alignment business that brings out the dark side of mechanics? Pay heed to the words of one mechanic I interviewed:

Our shop does almost everything but alignments so we wanted to add an alignment machine too. These days the 4-wheel types are fully computerized. They have to be, because you are dealing with so many different variables at the same time. The companies we dealt with wanted over $40,000 for the machine, plus a service contract. That's crazy. Most customers barely understand the need for this service, and the ones who do won't pay much above $30 or $40, tops. Just to break even on the machine, since we are a full-service shop, not just an alignment shop, we would need a steady series of bookings at about $40-$60 apiece. I asked around and found that other shops in our situation would buy the equipment, low-ball the advertised price to under $20, and then make sure that every customer buys about $500 of suspension parts whether they are needed or not. That's the only way to make money in alignment, unless you do it all day, and are booked *all day. We hated to do it, but we decided to forget the alignment machine.*

The Car Kung Fu tip from this story? First, be careful. Second, choose a shop that does alignments as a speciality, preferably for fleet and wholesale customers. Avoid any places that advertise great rates on this service: somebody will end up paying for the bargain, probably you!

A 4-WHEEL ALIGNMENT CHECK LIST

1. If your vehicle was manufactured after 1980, chances are it was meant to have all four wheels aligned at once. To verify, check the owner's manual or take the vehicle to any shop that has 4-wheel alignment equipment and ask what sort of alignment is required.
2. If your vehicle has recently been in an accident, regardless of make or year, a 4-wheel alignment is an excellent method to verify that the body work was done properly.
3. Four-wheel alignment is not a panacea. It will not correct problems caused by worn suspension parts or incorrectly balanced or badly inflated tires. All these must be corrected before a 4-wheel alignment can help.
4. In a harsh climate, a 4-wheel alignment should be done at least once a year or approximately every 15,000 km.
5. Four-wheel alignment machines are, themselves, subject to misalignment. Deal only with shops that have their equipment tested by the manufacturer at least once a year.
6. Four-wheel alignment requires special training. Deal only with shops that post training certificates from recognized institutions for the technicians who are working on your vehicle.

BATTERY BLUES

In days gone by, the only thing that placed a drain on the battery when the engine was off was the clock — assuming, of course, that you had a clock in the first place. Since the power draw of those clocks on older cars was minimal, it was possible to leave the vehicle unattended for several weeks at a time and return to find the battery still in relatively good health.

Today things have changed: modern cars use a large number of electronic doodads which store memory codes even when the engine is off. Typical examples are digital clocks and radios. When you turn your car on in the morning you expect the clock to have remembered the right time and you expect the radio to remember your favourite stations. *They do, but at a price.* The price is the power draw placed on your battery as you sleep peacefully through the night. Nor are radios and clocks the *only* things that have a power draw. If you have automatic climate control or memory seating, then *those* devices also draw on your battery

The battery and the computer are interdependent. Disconnect the battery even for few minutes and your car will forget it's a car!

Finally, the motor itself has a complex computer system which is designed to memorize engine malfunction "trouble codes" as they occur during normal use. The purpose of this feature is to make life easier for the diagnostic mechanic when you eventually bring your car in for service. But the intermediate result is bad news: more current draw. What to do about all this ? Not much you *can* do really. Either disconnect the negative battery terminal before leaving the car alone, or make an appointment for a boost start when you get back from long periods away. And welcome to the twentieth century!

By now you are starting to get the picture. The odds that your battery will live to a ripe old age under normal conditions are poor at best. Most batteries are legally dead after four years of use. But most motorists, trying to pull those extra few months of service from those worn out cells, keep their batteries approximately six years. No wonder those *extra* two years can get pretty adventurous, especially in chilly weather.

OK, you've now made the decision to replace the battery *before* trouble strikes. Where do you go? What brand do you favour? The fact of the matter is that all batteries are more or less the same. There are only a handful of battery manufacturers on the continent and they supply private label brands for just about everybody. Your best bet is buy on service, not on price. Look for a shop that will install your battery quickly and professionally while you wait. And one that will give you a warranty that you can live with. Over the last ten years, the Sears Diehard has consistently scored higher than most others in its class, so that is one brand to consider seriously. Another recent — and interesting — development is the invention of dual duty batteries which function remarkably like the old "piggyback" ballpoint pen refills of the '60s. If you inadvertently kill your battery, you simply pop open the hood and throw a switch which allows the reserve cells to take over from the dead ones. Currently only a few companies — like Interstate — offer this feature, but over the next years it is expected that all batteries will have this option.

DASHBOARD DEMONS

When people ask me for my wildest repair story, I usually tell them about the late-model American car in which the oil pressure warning light started to flash for no particular reason. The owner dutifully took the car to her mechanic. The mechanic dutifully checked all the pressure sensors and related doodads in the engine oil system and determined that they were functioning OK. But the dash light continued to flash on and off for no reason. Ergo, the problem must be the warning light itself, inside the dashboard. The problem was, on the new cars, the dashboards are just large circuits boards...with no moving parts. You have to replace them; you can't repair them. The mechanic put in a call to the manufacturer who confirmed the entire dash would have to be replaced. Cost of replacement, for a rebuilt dash, not a new one: $1,700. And before the stunned mechanic could react to *that*, the manufacturer's rep hit him with another bombshell: there was also a deposit required up front. The rebuilder needed time to determine whether the old dash was a suitable trade-in. The "refundable" deposit was $4,000, making the whole thing a grand total of $5,700, plus tax and labour.

The mechanic called the customer and explained the situation. He pointed out that, of the estimated $6,000 charge, some $4,000 would be likely be refunded when the old dash was received in good condition. As soon as the customer determined that the mechanic was serious, and that she was not on Candid Camera, she told the mechanic to disconnect the oil pressure light and she would take her chances. Even if an engine problem did develop, a new engine would cost as much as fixing the light.

This story is absolutely true, by the way, and it has two extra kicks to it which I want to draw to your attention. First, the mechanic in question was curious about what was inside this "non-repairable" dash so he opened it up anyway and found a loose screw which was the entire cause of the problem.

Second, this amazing old story is not really that old. I heard it just a few months ago and the car in question was only a 1985 model. So, here's the bottom line. Chances are the design of your own dashboard is not that much different from the design of the dashboard in this story. And if that doesn't keep you up nights, nothing will.

HEADLIGHT REPLACEMENT

First, let's review a little light bulb history. In the beginning, car headlights were of one type — ordinary filament — and generally of only two sizes: first, the big round ones, sold in sets of two, that looked like giant eyeballs; and then the smaller circular ones that acted as either high- or low-beam, sold usually in sets of four. Each bulb cost about $10. To change the bulb you needed a screwdriver. Period. Every garage carried spare bulbs. Life was simple. In the last few years life has become not so simple.

First, halogen-type headlights (lights made brighter by the presence of halogen gas) came out to replace the plain filament types. Halogen bulbs are themselves of two types: one type requires you to renew the inner lamp only, and the other type requires you to change the whole unit. Halogen bulbs, when they first arrived, cost three to four times what the filament type cost, but back then replacement was, overall, pretty simple. Well, time has marched on.

The newest style of headlight combines halogen bulbs with an outer customized lens. These wonderful units cost 10-25 times what the old-fashioned round units cost. If parts are worn or damaged, you may have to change the entire unit; there is no uniformity anymore from make to make. Oh —did I forget to mention that there is also no common set of instructions for changing these newer bulbs? It's a kind of Easter egg hunt. You look around until you find the screws which you *think* make the whole unit come loose, and then you undo those screws. If you guessed wrong, simply put the screws back and start over.

And if I mistakenly gave you the impression that you can use any garden variety screwdriver to make this repair, then let me apologize. The same clever people who designed these needlessly complex new headlamps have also designed a brand new, needlessly complex type of screw to keep them on the car. To work with these new $300 headlamps you need a new Torx screwdriver. About $15 at any hardware store. And guess what? Once you buy the Torx screwdriver, you won't be able to use it for anything else *except* changing your headlights. That's progress.

SPARK PLUG POINTERS

Just when you thought cars were finally becoming simpler and easier to maintain, along comes a new choice for you to make. Spark plugs. They now come in two flavours: regular and long-life. First, you have to remember that a spark plug is really not a very complex product. There are, please note, absolutely no moving parts. A spark plug is just, well, a spark plug. It is a place for the spark to travel through on its way to the inside of your engine — sort of an electronic road map, if you like. Still, the mere fact that the spark plug is simple doesn't preclude the spark plug manufacturers from spending millions of dollars to make it better. They did just that, and the result is plugs in regular and premium, the latter costing sometimes double or triple the price of the plain plug — in some cases up to $10 a plug or more.

What do you get when you buy a premium plug? First you get a very pretty plug, although since the plug goes inside the engine, this by itself is not really much of a plus. Second, you get slightly better starts, slightly better fuel economy, and a slightly smoother-running engine. The key word here is "slightly." Unless you drive to work with sensitive electronic digital measuring devices hooked to your engine, you are unlikely actually to notice any of these improvements.

So far, these premium plugs are starting to look like overkill, aren't they? But there is one major advantage. You also get super long life from these plugs. Most plugs today last about 40,000-50,000 km, but you might easily get 100,000 km from a set of premium plugs. Now the game gets more interesting: 100,000 km means that one set of plugs might last for as long as you own the car.

Still, considering the extra cost, are long-life premium plugs for everyone? The answer is probably "yes." They are sufficiently good value to justify buying them simply on their own. If, however, you have an engine with hard to reach plugs, where the installation is both complex and expensive, they make wonderful good sense. One spark plug change — for life. (Now, if they could only do the same thing with a tank of gas!)

BRAKES

Front brakes today are so different from those in cars of ten or even five years ago that it hurts in the pocketbook. Many cars showing up in mechanics' shops now show premature unbalanced wear in the front disc unit. The word "unbalanced" is important. These units, I am told, are wearing out because of inadequate assembly at the factory which causes unbalanced wear later on. The solution is to have the brake system checked early by a pro, even when there seems to be no problem.

One specialist I spoke to insists on doing one special servicing on his customer's front brakes within six months of receipt of the new vehicle from the dealer. The bushings and slides are relubricated, and the brackets and linings are removed and refitted for smooth operation. Lots of fluid is used to free up any sticky parts. Any rust, dirt or even rough edging from the factory assembly line is removed. This whole operation costs less than $100 but virtually guarantees full and even wear from the unit in years to come.

NOT NECESSARILY AN INSULT

If someone tells you your discs are undersized, that is not necessarily an insult. Car parts have changed a lot over the last few years — and not always for the better. Brakes are a good example. The disk/drum combinations introduced by the domestic makers in the late sixties were, with hindsight, quite wonderful. They stopped the car quickly. They lasted a long time between routine servicings. And they were almost impossible to damage or abuse. When those old brakes did finally wear out, usually you could get them back up to snuff with new pads only. Total cost under $100.

Now let's get back to reality. When the domestic and foreign manufacturers began to downsize their cars to save weight (and, therefore, improve fuel economy) they could not resist the temptation to tamper with systems that were already near-perfect. Like your brakes. On most modern cars, it is extremely easy to damage the front discs or rotors —that's the part that the pads make contact with when they stop the car. In fact, according to several mechanics I have interviewed, it is impossible *not* to damage these new downsized parts over time. Simple everyday driving will likely destroy them within the first three to four years of ownership. And the replacement cost is pricey: figure about $200, plus the normal cost of servicing the brakes and changing the pads. When the discs do wear out, by the way, the change is almost impossible to detect without expert examination of the parts involved. Special measuring equipment is required. What the equipment will usually show is that the disc or rotor has worn away relative to its original specification. In other words, it has become undersized. So, when someone tells you your discs are undersized, it's really not meant to be taken personally....

DISTRIBUTORLESS IGNITIONS

The same wonderful people who tirelessly slave away to bring you things like milkless ice-cream and eggless eggs have seemingly gotten together with the car companies to produce ignition systems that don't need distributors. Instead, the correct timing for the ignition discharge is triggered by electronic sensors cleverly hidden within the engine's camshaft. This is almost as clever as removing your watch from your wrist to have it surgically embedded in your spine. And just about as easy to fix. I still don't know what horrible crimes the old distributors were guilty of — they seemed to have kept humankind on wheels for about a century. But I'll wager than anyone who ever has to repair one of these new-fangled distributorless systems will cry a little tear or two for the old ways.

RADIATORS

Here's another lightweight part which is a tad more fragile than it perhaps needs to be. (Some cars use aluminium in the rad and cooling system: great for weight, but not known for durability.) Flush and fill the radiator about every two years or 25,000 km. If you skip this step, you may not get into a jam while you have the car — but the person who buys it from *you* will be needing a new rad!

If you choose to have this operation performed at a garage, you have to specify one of three methods. The first, requiring no special equipment, whether done at home or in a garage, is a simple drain and fill. Gravity does all the work. You simply drain out the old and pour in the new.

The second method, which, again, can be done either at home or in the shop, involves hooking a pressurized water hose into the system to flush out accumulated waste before you add new coolant. Your mechanic has a special tool for this. If you want to do it at home, you would likely use a garden hose and special $2 connector.

So far, so good. Now, there is a third method. And it can't be done at home at all.

The third method is called on-site recycling, and it involves hooking your radiator to something that looks like a heart-lung machine. A heart-lung machine for cars, that is. The big difference between this method and the other two methods is that, in this method, you don't add new coolant at all. In this method, your old coolant is chemically cleaned, recycled and reconditioned to be, more or less, as good as new.

I know what you are thinking: "Wow, re-using that old coolant will probably save me big bucks, right?" Wrong. In fact this method costs slightly *more* than the other methods. Now you're saying, "Boy, this method must be much *faster* than the other two methods." Nope. Not really. "Hey," you say, "this method must at least do a *better job* than the other two." Nope, wrong again. The most you can expect from this on-site recycling is as good a job as the other methods.

"Now," you ask, "since there seems to be no advantage but the cost is higher, what the heck is really going on here?" The answer, in a word, is environment. Recycling antifreeze while it's still in the car means that no one has to worry about pouring it down a drain and killing another piece of our already sick planet. This is such an important issue to many people that they are even willing to pay a little extra for a new way to change antifreeze that is really no better than the old ways. And do you know what? It's not such a bad idea, at that.

DOES ON-SITE RECYCLING WORK?

Some suggest that on-site recycling devices don't really do what they're supposed to. Says Gord Robertson, V.P. Auto Products, First Brands (the makers of Prestone): "We have done exhaustive testing of all the major on-site recycling systems. The first problem is that they don't really flush out all the old water-antifreeze mix. The second problem is that none of the systems we tested meets 'original equipment' (OEM) specs for new antifreeze. Some are better than others, but none matches OEM. But," Robertson cautions, "please don't get the idea that I don't like the idea of on-site recycling. In principal, I do."

Another point that Robertson likes to make is that antifreeze really isn't "just" antifreeze. It's actually a very complex chemical soup. To make matters even more interesting, not all the antifreeze "chefs" seem to agree on what goes into the soup. Manufacturers in Europe use a different chemical mix from those in North America. And the Japanese tend to use an altogether different chemistry from the first two. Of course, this does not pose a problem when you pour all fresh, new antifreeze from the same jugs. A problem arises, however, when you have to come up with a standard rejuvenating formula that will restore *all* antifreeze mixes for *all* cars and *all* makes (regardless of race, creed or origin, as some might say!). According to Robertson, this just can't be done.

Dan Falla at Dow Chemical, another major manufacturer of raw antifreeze, agrees completely with Robertson's criticisms of current on-site hardware: "Nothing meets OEM standards. That's all there is to it."

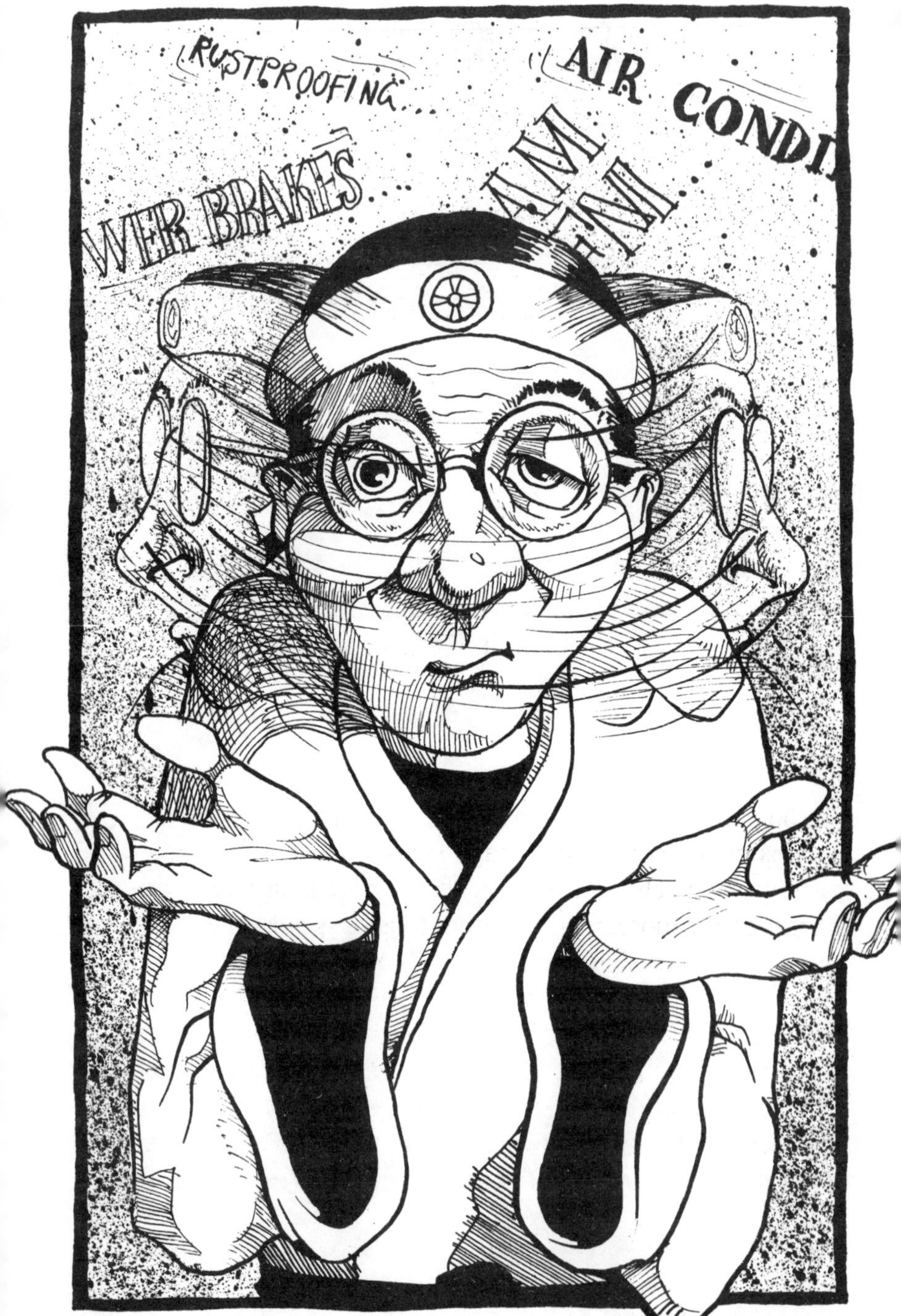
RUSTPROOFING
AIR CONDI
WER BRAKES
AM
FM

8

—

Bells And Whistles

New or used, cars come with a lot of bells and whistles. Some are optional, and some aren't. Here are some of the more interesting.

RUST-PROOFING

It bothers me that people still insist on referring to rust in terms of the cosmetic damage it does and not in terms of safety and mechanical damage. If you have a car that is seven years old or more, you may want to give special attention to what rust can do beyond merely poking holes in your fender. Recently a student called up because the lock on her driver's door wouldn't open. Taking the door apart I found that rust had sealed the locking mechanism almost completely shut. The only solution at this stage was either to change the parts (expensive!) or to lube the locking mechanism immediately, and then every six months subsequently, until the car was ultimately scrapped.

Another student was pleased as punch when she found an older Japanese car at a very good price. There was, however, a strange shimmy in the steering, which she figured an alignment would fix. Boy, was she surprised when the alignment mechanic told her the steering parts were so badly rusted that an alignment was literally impossible. In fact, since the subframe in this case had rusted as well, even a repair was impossible. Within days, the car was junked.

In the last few years I've had letters from a number of students who have been experiencing strange electrical problems with their cars. The symptoms never stayed the same. Sometimes a switch worked, sometimes it didn't. Sometimes a flasher flashed, and sometimes it just sat there. In each case, it took several hours of diagnostic time to trace the problem back to rust in the fuse-box. Once diagnosed, this was not too difficult to solve, however. A new fuse-box was usually enough to get the car going.

I can recall a Pontiac I owned that got harder and harder to start with each passing month. A half-dozen mechanics had tried to solve the problem and couldn't. Finally the culprit was revealed: a tiny smidgeon of rust under the bolt that fastened the negative battery post to the engine ground. The repair took only a minute to do.

And then there are the economics of corrosion. For most car owners, rust is the ultimate four-letter word. Even before your vehicle starts to depreciate, it starts to rust.

True, manufacturers are quick to point out that they are doing more to prevent rust today than at any other time in automotive history. First, they are designing cars with fewer internal crevices and cubby-holes where water and other foreign substances can collect and accelerate the corrosion process. Second, they are using a costly double-sided galvanized steel in their production process to further reduce rust's chances of gaining a toe-hold. And, third, they are pre-coating critical portions of the car's innards with waxy, rust-retarding substances prior to shipping, thereby cutting down even further the likelihood of rust getting a headstart on your vehicle.

These claims must be taken with a grain of salt. That new cars do, indeed, rust can be verified by visiting any automobile dealership and peeking down underneath the floorpan or gas tank areas. And, as far as that fancy steel is concerned, sure, it works — but it also costs the manufacturer significantly more to work with. As a result, the less expensive the car, the less generous the maker is likely to be with the galvanized or coated metals.

It may well be that today's new cars are rusting less, overall, because of these aggressive new anti-rust strategies. But the bottom line is that rust is inevitable. Just like death and taxes — you can postpone 'em, but you can't beat 'em.

What exactly is rust? First, consider corrosion as essentially an electro-chemical process. On a molecular level, the product of oxygen and metal — rust — is a more stable compound than the metal itself. It follows, therefore, that once rust gets a toe-hold, it is very difficult to stop.

Automobiles will rust whenever the right combination of elements exists to fuel the corrosion process. Naturally, the biggest source of available oxygen is good old H_2O — water. So if you could somehow keep water away from your vehicle you would never have rust. (Good luck!)

You may think that road salt causes rust, but that is only partly correct. Road salt tends to ionize, or speed up, the electrical portion of the corrosive process — much like adding salt to a pot of water makes it boil faster. Also, salt has a sponge or poultice effect. It attracts and keeps the water close to the metal, thereby giving the rust a lot of time, and opportunity, to get chummy with your car.

Condensation is a much bigger factor in rust than many people realize. Condensation on metal will occur any time there is an extreme range of temperatures experienced within a relatively short period of time.

For example, you may have noticed water forming on your windshield whenever you drive into a hot underground garage on a cold day. Now imagine that same condensation process taking place upon every square centimetre of sheet metal within your vehicle. It's invisible, but it is happening. You can't see it (unless you take a chain saw and cut open a fender) but your car undergoes this condensation cycle every morning when the sun comes up, and every time you move into a warm environment on a chilly day. (Trivia fans take note: this is why even California cars rust inside the panels, although the process is much slower than in the Northeast. Condensation is condensation, no matter where you live.)

This condensation theory explains why you see rust on parts of the car that are otherwise hard to get access to: inside trunk lids, around windshield pillars, in obscure corners of fenders, on the lower portions (but not the bottoms) of doors. It also explains what could be the biggest "mystery" in the rust-proofing business: why all the major shops specifically exclude the roof area in their warranties. Theoretically, the inside of the roof could be reached with the rust-proofing solution to prevent or reduce condensation damage. However, there is simply too great a risk of cosmetic staining caused by chemical interaction between the anti-rust solution and the car's fabric headliner.

Another conceptual problem with rust is its path of penetration. Stubborn owners persist in regarding rust bubbling as a surface problem. In fact, surface rust is just the opposite. (Contrary to what you may hear from your friendly neighbourhood rust-proofer should you ever try to make a claim on your warranty!) Virtually all visible rust starts beneath the panel and then works its way through. This is sometimes referred to as the "iceberg effect" because you are only seeing the tip of the problem. It also explains why exterior waxing has almost no preventative effect on car rust. If you want to prevent rust, you need rust-proofing. It's that simple.

But what type? Most rust-proofing sold today falls into two broad categories: the quick dry coating or sealant type, and the "gooey drippy" oil type. The former category is far and away the most popular with new car dealers, mainly because of its invisibility factor: buyers are charged upwards of $500 for something they can't see, feel or even inspect. (In fact, your half-a-grand often buys you about $20 worth of raw chemical and about 40 minutes of helter-skelter application.) The biggest irony of the quick-dry sealant is that no one really knows how useful it *might* be, because the application is generally so shoddy that rust will first take hold in the areas the applicator missed, and then slowly but surely undermine the areas that were actually coated. (This is easily verified by stopping at any wrecking yard and peering inside the panels of an older vehicle.) In fairness, the installer does not have an easy time of it. In most cases the rust-proofing material is applied "blind" through small access holes drilled into the body parts. Imagine trying to paint your living room while standing on the front porch and using a long brush!)

And then there is oil, a process first popularized in the Northeast and surprisingly hard to come by in the rest of the continent. The main benefit of giving your car's bottom and innards a bath in oil is that gravity (plus special additives in the oil) can work to move the stuff around inside your car's hidden crevices for days, weeks, or even months after the original job was done. Any spot missed by the technician during the original application will usually be caught when the stuff shimmies through the grillework while you sleep. Also, unlike the sealants, oil doesn't dry or crack over time. It's on the job 24 hours a day, repelling moisture and keeping your metal safe and protected. Also, the oil coating inside the panel will serve to slow down any minor rusting that is already underway, sometimes delaying the bubbling process for months or even years.

In a nutshell, oil works. Oiling can keep you rolling on winter's streets almost indefinitely.

But oil also drips. Boy, does it drip! The excess will seep off your car for weeks after the application, making a holy mess of your driveway or parking spot. And there's more. Some of that creepy crawly oil film will work its way onto the painted outer surfaces of the car and attract dirt like a magnet — unless you wash the car frequently, that is. And, the biggest drawback of all, oil doesn't last. All that moving back and forth wears it down over time. The oil coating must be completely renewed — at full cost — approximately every 12-18 months to keep the effectiveness up. (The warranties typically say once a year, but, if you don't mind taking a chance, you can probably get good results on an even longer cycle.)

Also, oil treatments are hard to find. In some places the only oil treatment you can buy is the one that goes inside your engine, not inside your body.

Trying to determine which of these two dramatically different processes is better may be difficult. Theoretically, the simpler (and tidier) sealant process will work adequately — provided, that is, you are prepared to take the car apart (literally!) in order to apply it properly. Oil processes, on the other hand, have demonstrated an almost blemish-free record in Europe and Canada, where they are most popular. But even that system's strongest proponents dread their annual appointment with the oiler, and the slimy drippy mess that inevitably follows.

TOO LATE?

What do you do if you have a car which is *already* rusted, and you aren't quite prepared to say goodbye to it just yet? Your options are few. First, the sealant processes won't work at all — they must be applied to new, clean metal to have any effect. Oil will help, but if the rust has reached the stage where the outer paint is peeling or bubbling then you are only buying yourself a little time before the inevitable happens. More than likely you need a body shop.

And not just any body shop at that. The vast majority of today's shops are used to fast, clean collision jobs where the bill is picked up by an anonymous deep-pocketed insurance company. Rust repair, on the other hand, is messy and very labour intensive. And, not surprisingly, the car owner generally wants to get the most value for the least money.

First and foremost, find a shop that really *wants* your business. Avoid shops that won't answer your questions or explain in detail what sort of repair they intend to make ("metal welding" is much preferred to fibreglass or plastic filler). Make sure that *all* the rust is covered in the estimate — it may be that nothing less than a full strip and repaint will be enough to get your car in proper shape again. Note also that you can protect your rust repair investment by treating the car promptly after it comes out of the shop. Floor or underbody work should receive a quick-dry sealant coating. Any other rust repairs need oil spray on the inner panels to keep the rust from coming back.

FOUR-WHEEL DRIVE

For many years, the vast majority of cars were 2-wheel drive, specifically the two wheels in the back of the vehicle. This arrangement, although not earth-shattering, was functional. It was known as rear-wheel drive. The Europeans were the first to realize that it was possible to increase interior roominess and, simultaneously, decrease overall vehicle weight by changing these design characteristics just slightly. They stayed with two wheels to move the car, only those two wheels were now the ones in the front. Makers like Renault, Audi and Saab showed that not only could this be done, it could be done with panache.

Although there were some small limitations to front-wheel drive (wear and tear was a little more severe and race track handling was hindered), overall, the twin goals of more space and less weight were achieved. There was also an added unexpected benefit: traction on slippery surfaces was drastically improved, although it was still possible to get stuck if the weather was bad enough. Nevertheless, front drive slowly but surely became an international standard. Four-wheel drive, where the engine moves all the wheels at once, was still considered too exotic for the average machine. The exceptions were trucks, jeeps and other speciality machines that had peculiar needs and could quickly switch from 2- to 4-wheel drive when needed. The idea of a 4-wheel drive vehicle that was driving four wheels all the time, even in normal weather, was crazy — until Audi developed the proper technology in the early eighties and showed how wonderful such a design could really be.

Today, other companies are copying this full-time 4-wheel-drive technology. VW, Toyota, GM, Subaru and Mazda are already selling models that have this feature. Other companies are following suit, although the form of 4-wheel drive they are offering may be slightly different. (Mercedes, for example, uses a more complex electronic system that is very computer-dependent. The 4-wheel power comes on only when needed, and not a second earlier, or later.)

Is all this fuss over 4-wheel drive really justified? You're darn tootin' right, it is. Although full-time 4-wheel drive costs you more initially, and may run up slightly higher repair bills over its lifetime, what you are really buying is an insurance policy that is hard to put a price on. Such a car is unlikely to ever again get stuck in snow or mud, and overall handling will be improved in all weather. The downside? Well, since most of these designs are new, we have to play with the data from the older Jeeps (which have been around since World War II in one form or another) to see what is really going on. It's not a happy prognosis. If the Jeep experience is any indicator, any form of 4-wheel drive technology will cost the owner buckets of extra money over the life of the vehicle. To minimize these costs, the owner merely has to follow — seriously — the maintenance schedule that came with the vehicle. (It usually involves regular inspections, lubrication and fluid changes for the 4-wheel drive hardware.)

FOUR-WHEEL STEERING

Is 4-wheel steering the best thing that happened to cars since stereo multiplex? Maybe. And maybe not.

First, some background.

Mazda, Nissan and Honda made history in 1988 by bringing out cars with 4-wheel steering, cars in which the rear wheels can steer in the opposite direction from the front ones. All these companies were at great pains to point out that the reason for this unusual technology was that, according to their test results, 4-wheel-steering cars were more stable in high speed manoeuvres and more nimble in day-to-day parking situations. When I test drove these cars, I found the effect was somewhere between pleasant and weird. I very seriously questioned whether the supposed benefits could justify the high initial expense and ongoing maintenance charges.

A while ago, 4-wheel steering faced its toughest challenge yet. A research project done at the University of Missouri in the late eighties concluded that the overall stability of a 4-wheel steering system was no better than that of a normal 2-wheel steering system. By stability, the researchers were referring to the ability of the average driver to control the car. This shocking study also raised a second even scarier finding. It concluded that, "if not properly maintained," the 4-wheel steering system might ultimately become even *less* stable than the normal 2-wheel steering system. What this means is that, if you didn't precisely follow the manufacturer's maintenance schedule, you may have ended up with a relatively *more* hazardous vehicle than the plain 2-wheel steering version.

This study, not surprisingly, was seriously challenged by all the makers of 4-wheel steering cars. I dug around, however, and discovered it agreed in principle with a prior study by a national car magazine in which 4-wheel steering cars were consistently out performed by 2-wheel steerers on both dry and slick pavement.

If that isn't enough to quell your lust for this obscure option, let me hasten to add that the extra parts needed to make 4-wheel steering a reality are expensive and wear-prone. And, outside of the friendly dealership, I don't know of any alignment equipment that can tell you, with accuracy, if your four wheels are still pointing in the same general directions they were when they left the factory. (You may at this point be wondering what 4-wheel steering feels like, I'll bet. I will tell you two things. First, the feeling is so hard to differentiate from regular steering that it takes some time to realize that anything unusual is actually happening. Then — this from a Honda Prelude 4-wheel-steerer I tested — it suddenly dawns on you that the rear of the car is acting more like a boat than a car. You turn the rudder — ah, excuse me, steering wheel — and the car seems to pivot midpoint in its zeal to make the turn. Fun, yes. Worth $5,000 extra? I really don't think so.)

RADIOS AND WHATNOTS

To say that the domestic industry missed the boat on sound systems is like saying they missed the boat on small cars, reliability and value. All statements are true. Or, at least, *were* true until approximately the mid-eighties. Until that time it was a safe bet that any aftermarket radio purchased anywhere other than the dealer would outperform the manufacturer's offerings — and usually for less money, at that.

In recent years the gap has narrowed. Now the radio and sound systems offered by the dealers, although a little pricey, are quite competitive. And, of course, if you order from the dealer when the car is new, you avoid the hassle of having someone uprooting seats and removing interior trim to make the installation. Most makers do offer a "pre-wire" option on new cars. This inexpensive option lets you buy a car with all the wiring in place — but nothing else. This makes it much easier to install an aftermarket sound system, if that is what your little heart is really set on.

What if you already have a sound system but want to "upgrade"? First, you really do need a bit of cash. Good sound systems cost dough, so figure on at least $500-$800, minimum, to upgrade yours to something that is state of the art. Second, you must have a good installer. I cannot emphasize this strongly enough. Radio installation is literally a lost art. Just because a store says it can install, doesn't mean it actually can. So ask around, and find an installer with credentials: a shop that can give you a list of satisfied customers.

The next question: Will the new system fit in the space taken by your old system? The answer is yes and no. There are a number of standard fits in the car radio business, and you should choose your new system only after carefully measuring the size of your old one and consulting with your installer. I'll repeat that. *Before* you buy, talk to your installer and make sure you're on the right track.

If worse comes to worst, a skilled technician can, sometimes, fit in an oversized system and make it look like it's factory original — but there are no guarantees.

What about speakers? On 90% of all cars on the road today, the speakers are junk. So when you do your budgeting, figure on replacing your present speakers with better ones, or you won't be able to appreciate the new system that you are installing. The only thing to watch out for during installation is rust: if the doors or rocker panels on your car are rusted, have a serious chat with the installer before approving the work. Installing equipment in or near rusty metal may make things worse. Aside from that, and assuming you can find a technician who is willing and able to do the proper job, your brand new improved sound system is just a few dollar— and a few decibels — away.

CAR BRAS

Interested? For about $100 dollars you can get a large, exquisitely tailored black automotive undergarment which is difficult to both install and remove. If your car has fliptop headlights, as some do, you had better get the installation just perfect the first time or risk damaging the headlights when you turn them on. The material does protect from small stone chips, but not big ones. A large rock or brick can, in my estimation, still penetrate the fabric and mess up the paint pretty smartly. Pollution and sunlight will also do unflattering things to your car's "undies" over time.

And, as for maintenance, what can I say? The bra I tested didn't seem to shrink or change colour after laundering — but I can't be positive because I only went through the car wash once. (It wasn't money I ran out of. It was courage.)

LIFETIME BATTERIES

No battery will last forever. All those recharge cycles that occur during normal driving can take their toll over the years. Still, this doesn't mean that no one will sell you a lifetime battery. Like a lifetime muffler, a lifetime battery is really a good battery with a great guarantee.

Let's review battery basics for a moment. Contrary to popular belief, a battery is useful only for starting your car. In other words, you could yank the battery out of a car with the engine already running — and nothing would happen! The engine would continue to run. However, once you shut that engine off, that would be it. No more engine unless you got a battery to start it.

Overall, then, your battery has a simple life — and a relatively long one. Most batteries will last about four or five years before old age sets in. And that's the key: when the battery starts to feel its age, that's the time to take steps to make sure you get started on cold mornings. What steps? A new battery of course. Nowadays a new battery will cost anywhere from $50-$150 dollars. At the low end you get a battery that will work ... for a while, and a guarantee that will protect you ... also for a while. At the top end, in the $150 class, you usually get a battery that is guaranteed for life, no excuses, period, end of story. My advice is that the more expensive battery is clearly the better buy. You get a double benefit: a higher quality battery to start with, and insurance against having to replace it in the foreseeable future.

Now the core issue: Are lifetime batteries really good enough to last forever? Of course not. However, these batteries do represent the latest in battery technology and, as I said, the warranties may be even tougher than the battery itself. Generally speaking, if the battery should fail, you pop down to the place where you got it and simply pick up a new one. In today's rough-and-tumble consumer marketplace, that's not really a bad deal at all.

TIRES

There are three things you should know about tires:

1. Although most drivers aren't aware of it, tire (and rim) technology is so advanced that an entire book could be written on the subject.

2. Contrary to what you may expect me to tell you, all tires are not all alike. Different combinations of brands, sizes and rim constructions can make an enormous difference in the way the car's suspension and braking system respond.

3. Finally, for 99% of all drivers, most of the information in #1 and #2 above can be ignored.

Almost all buyers today know and appreciate the superiority of radial tires, so I will spare you that particular sermon. (This was not the case as recently as ten years ago, however.) What is often unappreciated are some of the other factors involved in choosing tires and wheels:

*   Those fancy alloy wheels are not meant for show only, although, practically, that's why most folks buy 'em. By reducing the "unsprung weight" of the vehicle, they enhance the performance, steering and braking characteristics of the car. Your car. Any car. No matter. On the downside, they are costly to buy and hard to both install and maintain. They are also the equivalent of economic suicide if you intend to drive them through salt or snow.

*   The average car, whether foreign or domestic, can handle as many as a half-dozen combinations of tire size and rim size. Of course, only a tire store expert would be able to explain this to you. If you ask the new car salesperson you may get back only a blank stare for your trouble. As a rule, you should go with whatever numbers the manufacturer of the car recommends. However, if you must fiddle, keep the following in mind: lower, wider tires deliver better overall performance in dry and slightly wet weather. In deep snow or ice, however, thinner, smaller tires seem to perform better.

ATTENTION NEW-CAR BUYERS

One thing that has not changed at all in the last 50 years of the car business is that the tires that come "standard" on the new car you buy are likely to be the least tire for the most money. Not that they may be dangerous. Far from it. Just that, unless you make a fuss, you can expect the minimum from your dealer rubber, not the maximum. And don't try to discuss this with that salesperson! Chances are he'll be too busy trying to get you to take the paint/sealant/rust-proofing package to worry about tires. My advice is simple: if you are spending the money on a new car anyway, drive right from the dealer to a tire specialist. (By this I mean a company that does most of its business with tires and rims, not companies like Goodyear and Firestone that sell tires alongside their service bays.) Ask for a recommended wheel rim and tire package for your vehicle, then ask for something as a trade back for the dealer stuff that's already on there. If you don't like the numbers, of course, get another quote from another shop. The point is, good rubber can dramatically improve the safety and handling of your vehicle. And the best time to make the move is when the car is factory-new.

- All-season radials are the best all-around choice for most people. In harsh winter climates, nothing is as good as true winter radials on all four wheels.

- Just to make your life more interesting, some makers of tires sell the same model under different names (these usually turn up in chain stores). Knowing this can help get you a deal if you shop carefully. (Hint: Sears often has Michelin make its line. Michelin almost never puts it own tires on sale, but Sears has sales with each change of the seasons.)

Is there any easy way to figure out what quality you are really buying? The answer is, surprisingly, already on the tire, in the form of three test specifications which US federal law requires to be in plain sight. All you have to is read it! Look for three rating categories: heat dissipation, traction and treadwear. The first two categories, heat dissipation and treadwear, are marked like a grade school report card. A is great, B is OK, C is rotten. This specification is not required by Canadian law, but about 60% of tires sold in Canada come from the US.

Heat dissipation, by the way, is the ability of the tire to avoid blowing out even when underinflated or run at high speeds. And traction, just as it says, is the ability of the tire to move the car in all kinds of weather. The third rating, treadware, is a bit trickier to read. Look for a three-digit number between 100 and 250. Without going into all the mathematics, 100 is poor, 250 is great, and 175 is about normal.

Most, but not all, tires have these numbers engraved on them. Conversely, few tire salespeople, if any, will mention these numbers to prospective purchasers. The reason is that, until recently, most of the better known tire brands had rotten ratings, while the lesser known imported brands tended to show better ratings. This situation has changed a bit in the last few years, however.

Right now you're probably wondering whether you have to pay a premium to get tires with a better rating. The answer is an amazing *no*. Because these ratings are so little known, the tire companies shamelessly charge as much for rotten tires as they do for the good ones. One the other hand, now that you know this secret, you can, by being a Car Kung Fu practitioner, choose a tire model with great specifications and pay no more than you would for any other tire.

How long should a tire really last? The answer is, "It depends." In the US, the results of a recent study on tire wear found that the type of driving you do and the type of vehicle you own are by far the biggest factors in tire wear, all other things being equal. In tracking the wear of the same brands of tires on different vehicles and in different uses, the study found that police car use — considered as severe service — wore out tires in under 20,000 miles or about 35,000 km. Business or fleet owners got about 30,000 miles from their rubber, or about 50,000 km. And average drivers who just used their vehicles to go to and from the job pulled in about 35,000 miles of service from their tires, or about 60,000 km.

Keep in mind, when examining these numbers, that basic preventive maintenance was included in the test. For example, tire pressure was checked every few weeks and air added if necessary. As you may know, underinflated tires can reduce tire life by a shocking 30-40%. Also, proper alignments were done about every eight months. Proper, in this case, means that, if the car required the fancier and more costly 4-wheel alignment, then that's what it got. (Most cars on the road today, by the way, do require the fancy 4-wheel type of alignment.)

The other factor to keep in mind when considering tire wear is warranty performance. Some, but not all, tires sold today include a guaranteed wear cycle. If, for example, your tire is guaranteed for 60,000 km and, in spite of proper maintenance, the tire gives up the ghost at only 50,000 km, then you can return to the dealer where the tire was originally purchased and receive a credit toward the cost of a new tire.

Most of these types of guarantees do not allow you simply to *replace* the old tire for a new one, nor do they allow you cash back on the warranty. All you get is a credit toward the purchase of new tire — period.

Finally, here's a tip which may help some of you before trouble strikes. I have noticed many late-model cars on the streets using, on one wheel, those small space saver spare tires which were developed back in the seventies to save trunk space. Apparently, some owners have assumed that a spare is a spare is a spare, and are using these things in place of a regular tire that has gone bad. *Stop it!* These wimpy rubber donuts are meant for emergency short-term use only. They can't take day-to-day driving. If you leave one on the car for any length of time, you are asking for trouble.

WAXES AND POLISHES

I wish I had a dollar for every time someone asked me whether or not those lifetime waxes really work! Anyway, my answer has not changed at all over the years. Lifetime wax is great marketing backed by a poor product. It is the nature of paint to dull over time when exposed to the elements, and it is in the nature of waxes to deteriorate over time as well. Most so-called sealants operate on the notion that, at a microscopic level, tiny imperfections in the paint surface allow outside contaminants a better chance to do their damage. By sealing or smoothing the surface, the sealant will, so the theory goes, give the paint greater protection and make it more durable.

True? To a degree. But the fact remains that, as in the case of the notorious dealer rust-proofing packages, what you are really buying, for your $500, is still only $15 worth of chemical and about 45 minutes of application. And while the warranty seems to promise perpetual glossiness, in the fine print you will find 1,001 reasons why you might have to come back every now and then for a retreatment.

It's cheaper — and smarter — simply to pick a good product off a store shelf for under $10 and apply it yourself. Over the last decade or so, two commercial products have consistently had top ratings in independent consumer tests: Nu-Finish and Rain Dance.

INSURANCE

For as long as there have been cars, there have been car accidents. And for as long as there have been car accidents, there have been insurance companies to make things right again. At least in theory. Yet, year after year, I hear from dozens of students who have the most grisly stories to tell about car insurance companies. Let's take a typical example (although it may not apply directly to you if you live in a no-fault jurisdiction). You are waiting at a stop sign and suddenly another car thumps you from behind. Clearly the fault is not yours. You go to your own garage and are quoted $2,000 for the repair. You put a claim in under your own insurance policy.

You ask your insurance company for a check for $2,000, pretty please.

"Not so fast," they say. "We have looked over the estimate and we think it is too high. We have found another garage that will do the job for $1,500."

"Wait a minute," you scream. "I trust my garage; I don't trust strange garages."

"No deal," says the insurance company. "Take the $1,500 or leave it."

You are fed up and decide to give in.

"Gimme the $1,500 in cash," you say, "and I'll go to my garage and pay the difference myself."

"Not so fast," says the insurer. "If you want cash, then we'll assume you are really going to do the work yourself and we'll deduct something for the saving in labour. If you really want cash, we'll give you only $1000!"

Now things are really getting stupid. What started off as a $2,000 accident has become a $1,000 take-it-or-leave-it negotiation. And your insurance company is supposed to be on *your* side!

I wish I could give you an easy solution to this problem, but I can't. You might hire a lawyer or go to Small Claims Court. In almost every instance where policy holders have taken their own insurer to court over issues like this, the courts have ruled that the insurer must cover the full amount of the damage, regardless of when and where the work is done.

The good news is that these are your rights.

The bad news is that you may have to fight for them.

Now let's examine an even more typical situation. You get into another accident with your own late-model car. Again, let's assume that you go directly to your own insurance company for an immediate repair and let them fight it out with the other person's insurance company, if need be. Suppose the damage is so severe that you are concerned that the car may be a total write-off. "No need to panic," says your friendly insurer. "We have examined the car and we can fix it. Here's the garage to take it to. "

Grateful beyond description, you take the car to the specified garage and the insurance company pays for everything (except the deductible, if you have one). The car looks wonderful. Then, a few weeks later, doubts begin to set in. The car doesn't seem to keep in a straight line on the highway. The front tires are wearing badly and alignments don't seem to help. When you brake, the car pulls to one side. And the fan belts on the engine seem to be wearing out extra fast. Suddenly you realize you have a problem!

In the last few years I have personally looked into a half-dozen cases exactly like this so I can assume that there are likely thousands more out there in the same predicament. The problem is that serious damage to front-drive unibody vehicles is hard to repair properly in the first place. Second, most insurance companies, interested mainly in saving money, apply pressure to the repair shop to keep costs down, so now you have two strikes against you. Finally, if the repair is done wrong the first time — and if off-brand or used, substandard parts are employed — you don't really get a second chance. Once the metal is welded, it is very hard to reweld. That's three strikes — and you're out.

The solutions? One, pay extra for a "replacement value" policy (ask your insurance company for details). Two, check the credentials of any body shop you patronize, to make sure that workers there have the skill and expertise to fix your car properly the first time. (Look for what's called a "unibody alignment machine" and a certificate that someone knows how to use it.) Three, refuse to sign the insurance company's waiver until you have had a few months of driving to make sure your car really is as good as new. None of these options is especially easy or practical, I admit. But the alternative, I assure you, can be even worse.

GASOLINE

These days, if you have a car that uses leaded gas, you can't help but feel just a little paranoid. Every time you turn around someone reminds you that the days of leaded gasoline are numbered. Does this mean that you will have to trade cars? Or perhaps swap engines? Or use lead-free gas knowing that, in the process, you are possibly destroying your vehicle? Not necessarily.

First, let's look at why lead is in gasoline in the first place. Lead has two very special properties that make it useful in an internal combustion engine. First, lead has certain lubrication qualities. A car that burns leaded gas will benefit from better *lubrication* in the valve area and, in fact, many cars designed for leaded gas rely upon their fuel intake to lubricate the valves. We'll come back to this point in a moment.

Second, lead is one of the cheapest ways to raise the octane rating of gasoline, so that higher-compression engines can be used. Higher-compression engines are also higher-efficiency engines. They allow the smallest possible engine to produce the largest amount of horsepower. But a high-compression engine needs a high-octane gasoline and, until recently, that meant the use of lead.

Unfortunately, lead is also a poison. For the environment, for people, for everything. As governments became more aware of this aspect of lead, the gas companies went looking around for a lead substitute which would raise octane as well as lead does. They found one. This new lead substitute is now in virtually all the lead-free gasolines on the markets. The substitute costs more than lead to make, so lead-free gas initially cost more than leaded.

But what about lubrication qualities in lead-free gas? The lead substitute does not lubricate the upper valve area as well as lead, itself, does. The good news, however, is that virtually all engines built since 1973 are specially reinforced in the valve area to run without lead. So the bottom line is that if you have a car built since 1973, you're OK. If your car model is earlier than 1973, lead-free gas may hurt. But, realistically, if your car model is earlier than 1973 you should be happy it's running in the first place. The kind of gas you use may well be the least of your worries! (Some no-leads, by the way, claim that their blend will be correct even for pre-'73 cars.)

More recently another issue has come to the fore which makes putting gas into your tank a much more complex issue than it need be. Fuel-injection systems can clog if the proper additives are not used to keep the injectors clean. You have two options. Either check with your manufacturer to see what brand names of gasoline are currently ranked as having sufficient quantities of the right additive (your owner's manual may help here too); or regularly add a store-bought additive made especially to clean fuel injectors.

9

Behind The Wheel

It is a peculiarity of our culture that, while everyone wants to sell you a car, no one wants to take a moment to explain how cars work. Or how to work them.

The owner's manual, seemingly written almost entirely by lawyers, is not much of a help — though it can be surprising, and even amusing. I recall an owner's manual for a Jaguar which explained how the hand brake could be used in an emergency to slow down the car. It then went on to suggest that it might be a good idea to practise stopping the car with the hand brake a few times while the main brakes were still in working order. A good idea, but I can't quite picture a typical Jaguar owner on a deserted side street, hitting 90 km/h and then trying to stop the car with only the hand brake — can you?

Another memorable owner's manual was the one that came with a VW Passat. Under the towing section, in small print, it explained that the recommended maximum tow weight for the Passat was a hefty 2,000 lbs, an impressive number. However, the tinier print revealed, if you happen to have a Passat with an automatic transmission, that the maximum towing capacity dropped to 1,000 lbs. Try as I could, I was unable to imagine the look on the face of the buyer who shelled out extra dough for the automatic, only to find that he was now unable to tow his boat to the cabin for the summer!

Confused? Mystified? Upset? That's where Car Kung Fu comes in. In this chapter we look at some typical dash instruments and controls to discover what they really mean. (Note: Your car may not have all the gauges described below, and may use idiot lights for some. If so, I urge you to spend a tiny amount of money — usually under $50 — and have an auto electric expert install a gauge package. It is, I promise you, a bargain in the long run!)

OWNER'S MANUAL: A HELP OR A HOOT?

For years I have been saying that the owner's manuals that come with the new cars are almost impossible to read. The last time I looked, about 40% of the text in the average owner's manual was bold-faced warnings and cautions. These are written, for the most part, by lawyers. The reason they are written is *not* to tell you how to use the car, but rather to keep you from suing when you do use it and something bad happens. Only one problem — with all this legal garbage in these books, there is no room for useful information. Anyway, lately it seems I'm not the only who sees the big picture. A recent Washington-based study using consumer focus groups determined that, ta-dah, owner's manuals had reached a pretty lowly state indeed. As a result, in most manuals that will be produced through the nineties, we should expect fewer warnings and more explanations. The bad news? If you don't intend to buy a new car in the near future, you're stuck with your old manual, probably still in your glovebox, which is more or less the same pain in the fuel tank it always was.

HOT ENOUGH FOR YOU?

This may not make me too popular, but I will wager that you do not have a clue as to how your car's heater works. Every year, as winter reaches its peak, millions of North Americans poke and prod at their heater controls, trying to find a temperature that makes them cozy. Ever notice that there are two levers that seem to promise heat? One, with lots of cute little pictures, is meant for air direction. And that other, with the icy-cold blue and hot red symbols, is meant for temperature. What do they actually do? How do you use them in combination? All right, let's start with the basics.

First, it is important to distinguish the control that sets the air temperature from the control that sets the air direction or venting. The temperature or blend control is the one that has a range from hot to cold. On most cars it is not anywhere near as sophisticated as the thermostat in your home. What it does is adjust the blending of cool air from outside the car with hot air piped in from your car's radiator system (actually a small radiator under your dash called a heater box). In principle, it works like the adjusting tap in your shower. With practice you can usually find the right blend of hot and cold that works for you.

But where is this wonderful blend of air to be sent? That's where the other control comes in, the one with all the pretty pictures. The picture that points to your head does not mean that you were smart to buy the car. It means that cool outside air is being sent to your head. This control, by the way, will override the blend control. Even if the blend is set to hot, sending air to your head results in cold air, period.

The picture that points to your knees does not mean you have cute knees. This is the heater pictograph on the newer cars. With this setting, the blend control will override the direction control. If you choose knees and a cold blend, you get no heat. Tough. Now the easy part. The picture that shows knees and face means you get both cold outside air to your face and hot engine air to your knees. Needless to say, in subzero weather, this is not a smart idea as the two tend to cancel each other out. And the final setting, the picture of the window, is the defroster. It's easy. You use it to see where you're going when you can't see where you're going.

GAS GAUGE

The most important bit of information you can extract from this gauge is where "empty" is. Think about it. When you have the least gas, that's when you most need this gauge. And the information you want most is not how much gas you've used, but how much you have left. On most gauges, you can figure this out simply by turning the engine off and seeing where the needle drops to. (Some cars have what I call the "vampire" feature: even after power is cut, the gauge stays alive, faithfully reporting on fuel availability. On these you will never know where empty really is, until it's too late!)

TEMPERATURE GAUGE

Even in the absence of a malfunction, your car can run too hot or too cold. For reasons which escape me, a great many cars built in the eighties usually ended up emerging from a servicing with the incorrect thermostat installed in the cooling system. An alert owner can spot the problem by watching the gauge: the car will seem to take longer to reach normal operating temperature. (Running cold on the wrong thermostat ruins fuel economy, increases engine wear and hurts performance.) If you suspect your mechanic of installing a wrong thermostat, simply go back and ask him to re-install.

A much more serious situation is a hot engine. Most engines on the road today are no longer made of "Detroit iron." Instead, they have alloys like aluminium in them that are very heat-sensitive. In my estimation, driving 10 km with an overheated engine could cost you $250 in possible repairs! (Often, the damage will not turn up until months after the overheating.)

THIS COULD BE YOU

Ron joined the course after a particularly bad experience. He had just paid over $7,000 for a late-model VW Camper which seemed to be in excellent condition. Less than a week after purchasing the vehicle, a water hose blew and the engine began to overheat. Ron immediately noticed the overheat condition, but figured there could be no harm in driving the extra few kilometres home. A block from his destination the engine seized. The dealer quoted him $4,000 to rebuild the engine. After he had taken my course, I sent him to a private mechanic who was able to reuse many original parts from the old engine, including some of the pistons. The cost was just slightly over $2,000. While the vehicle was in the shop, the owner asked Ron if he knew about the "peculiar exhaust system" on the car. "What peculiar exhaust system?" asked Ron. The owner pointed out that the entire exhaust was really a series of pieces cobbled together from other cars and welded in place. The heart of the system was a Fiat muffler, in fact. The system, although ugly, was functional. Still, the diligent owner asked Ron whether he wanted the proper exhaust parts put back in. "What will that cost?" asked Ron. "About $2,000" said the owner. Suddenly, it was clear why the former owner used non-original parts. Ron left the exhaust as it was and made sure that he kept good notes on how to check out the next used car he purchased!

OIL-PRESSURE GAUGE

High oil pressure is theoretically possible, but extremely uncommon. Low oil pressure is more likely. Low pressure can be chronic or acute. Chronic low oil pressure is usually the result of a seriously worn engine. In this case, the gauge is merely confirming what you already know: your engine needs help. (Strange engine noises, weird smells, high oil consumption and power loss have likely preceded the low pressure reading on the gauge.)

It is normal for oil pressure to dip slightly when idling and at stop signs. On a cold morning the oil pressure may take a few minutes to build up. An oil pressure problem, however, is a sudden loss of pressure that could be caused by a number of mechanical factors. Driving a car with low oil pressure is even more dangerous than driving an overheating car, if that is possible. Stop the car! Get out! Call a tow!

STILL MORE BANANAS IN THE CRANKCASE

Yes, it is true, chronic low oil pressure can be remedied for a few months by commercial oil thickeners like STP or Engine Honey. These treatments are liquid band-aids and are, at best, temporary. Avoid them in cold climes because the extra viscosity may make the engine hard to start. Bananas will also work, but are more likely to foul the plugs. And your engine doesn't really need the extra potassium, either.

VOLTAGE GAUGE

The trouble with these is that the normal reading produced by a healthy engine varies substantially during the day, depending on outside temperature, battery health, engine speed and the number of accessories, including lights, that are in use. Some makers compound the problem by installing the gauge, but not marking acceptable ranges — so the driver has a pretty needle to watch but no idea of what to watch *for*.

Your best bet, if you have one of these, is to familiarize yourself with the range of movement when the car is obviously healthy and the battery is new. Then, if the needle seems to dip too low or too high later on, get the car checked.

Also keep in mind that a dangerously low voltage will often be accompanied by other warning signs. For example, the dash gauges may get very dim, the horn may sound anaemic, or the headlights may not seem as bright as they should be.

An overcharging system — one that is overproducing — will give itself away by burning the battery and forcing you to add water on a regular basis. (Unfortunately, most newer batteries are maintenance-free, so by the time you know the system is burning the battery, it's too late. The battery is gone!)

One final tip: One of the hidden benefits of a voltage gauge — so well hidden that many manuals omit it — is that the gadget can be dual-duty. You may use it when the engine is running, as was intended, and you can also use it when the engine is off. In the former case, the gauge will do its 9-5 job; i.e., keep you informed of problems in the charging system. When used with the engine off (you turn the ignition key just enough to activate the gauge but not enough to start the engine), it gives you a good indication of the state of your battery. Used in this manner, the reading must be at least 12.5 volts.

What's more, if you really want to impress everyone with your Car Kung Fu lessons, try using the gauge a third way: to imitate the battery load test for which garages may charge as much as $25. It's simple. Use the gauge as in the second example above, but, this time, twist the key a little more and actually start the engine while watching the gauge carefully. If the voltage drops below 9 volts, you have a starting system problem (usually, but not always, a battery that is getting a bit long in the tooth).

CHECK ENGINE — MORE THAN A LIGHT, LESS THAN A GAUGE

This light suffers from a serious case of understatement. The check engine light is wired directly into your ECM or computer. It flashes, generally, when there is a "soft" or "hard" failure of a component in the computer system. (A "soft" failure is a temporary or occasional failure. A "hard" failure means the component or sensor is gone, gone, gone.) The light will also come on, and stay on, when your car goes into limp-in mode. Although the rules vary from model to model, it usually takes the hard failure of at least one major component in the system to activate limp-in. You will know you are in limp-in because, first, the check engine light will come on, and, second, the car will behave very strangely indeed. There will be no acceleration or power to speak off. (Note also that, unlike Check Engine, which — as I have said — smacks of understatement, limp-in seems very well named.)

10

The Most Dangerous Part Of The Car: You

The public, including the insurance companies and the law enforcement agencies, is just beginning to realize that the most dangerous part of the modern motorcar is the part behind the steering wheel. Not the design of the brakes, not the design of the suspension, but, rather, the design of the driver!

Please take me seriously.

Since the early sixties I have driven a great number of cars in major cities all over the world. And what I have seen scares the stuffing out of me.

Most major roadways, highways and traffic arteries now in use were built or designed at a time when the number of licensed cars (and drivers) on the road was much lower than it is now.

Ironically, as any city planner will attest, these roadways were barely adequate at the time of their original construction. Today — and this true for all major North American centres — they are a bad joke. And a dangerous one.

THE SCARIEST STATISTIC OF ALL

A major magazine did a survey and discovered that over two-thirds of all drivers think that bad driving habits are the most serious problem on modern highways. The same survey also found that over three-quarters of all drivers rated their *own* skills as excellent. Some even suggested that they would have picked a higher category than "excellent" if one had been offered.

What's wrong with this picture, folks?

If you want proof, just get in the car and drive anywhere during rush hour. You'll see. Bumper-to-bumper traffic belies the supposedly synchronized signal lights. The result, most often, is long waits and short tempers.

Cars have, over the last few decades, become much smaller and much more nimble. Today irate drivers, on the spur of the moment, can attempt — and I use the word advisedly — manoeuvres that would have been impossible a generation ago. In the sixties, when everyone drove cars the size of skating rinks, social scientists noted in passing that drivers of VW Bugs, though they lacked power, had the nimbleness to dart in and out of traffic, and generally make everybody else on the road wish them ill. Statistically, Bugs were a small percentage of the total population at the time, so people tolerated them. Today, over 75% of all cars on the road meet or exceed the nimbleness of the old Beetle.

In point of fact, most cars on the road today achieve degrees of performance that are astonishing by older yardsticks. In 1989, while doing my "best of breed" for a radio program, I gave my Car of the Year award to the Toyota Corolla. My reasons were:

- good price;
- many standard features;
- excellent repair and reliability record;

- comfortable roomy chassis, excellent handling and ride;
- nice looks;
- and — more than anything — a four-cylinder engine, standard on this "family" car, which was able to meet or exceed the performance of many sixties muscle cars.

OK, we know what the cars can do. But what about the drivers? Friendly, social-minded, caring folk, you say? Hardly. On the heels of the "me" generation, we have a bunch of drivers on the road whose idea of courtesy is a three-second warning before they attempt to run you into a lamppost.

Yes, I am stretching things a bit, but my thesis — that today's roads and today's drivers are more dangerous than ever — is borne out by the facts. In spite of the fact that today's cars are theoretically safer than ever before, the number of accidents, fatal and otherwise, is on the increase.

If it's not the cars, folks, it must be the drivers. And I think it is.

Today's drivers in all parts of North America have a minimum of training when they first get behind the wheel. This sad, simple truth is attested to by the fact that the vast majority are completely ignorant of the #1 rule of road safety: If you are not looking to pass, stay in the right lane.

This rule and others like it (explained below) are not new. In fact, in most jurisdictions in North America, it is actually a traffic offence to stay in the left lane for no particular reason. Still, most drivers are clued out. Dangerously so. And, if most drivers are ignorant of this, the most basic rule of road courtesy, what do they know of the more subtle stuff, the stuff we look at in Car Kung Fu?

Nothing. Less than nothing.

Maybe "minus nothing."

THE CAR KUNG FU ROAD SAFETY RULEBOOK

Let's look at a few driver skill basics.

1. If in doubt, get in the right lane.

If you are at all involved in car politics, the whole question of left-lane hogging has become as highly charged as any social issue. Simply put, most people ignore the "stay in right lane" rule because:

- They don't know it.
- They believe — incorrectly — that it is for high-ways only. In fact, it applies to any roadway with more than one lane!
- Traffic is so congested they somehow feel that the open spot in the left lane is just what they have been looking for.
- They think they are somehow safer in that nice wide-open roomy left lane. (Wrong! See below.)
- They have come to be convinced that it is their moral duty to stay in the left lane going the legal limit and, in the process, prevent evil speeders from creeping past them.

It is, sad to say, the last category that causes most of the trouble and, I believe, a large number of accidents or, at least, near-accidents. That such vigilantes exist is not speculation. I have seen their letters to the editor in newspapers and magazines all around the country. The truth is that, for some unfathomable reason, their sense of moral outrage is activated by people who speed past them. They feel it is their personal crusade to enforce the law and "plug" the lane, even if it kills them. And sometimes it does. (Just for the record: while speeding is illegal, so is staying in a passing lane for purposes other than passing. Nobody wins here, folks.)

Yes, I admit it, there really are a lot of speeders out there who seem to have no other purpose than to run you, and other God-fearing folk, off the road. But, why take risks you don't have to? All the speeders and crazies generally drive in the extreme left lane *only* — so, as a general rule, stay in the right-most lane of the street or highway you're on, and you will have handily eliminated a major cause of accidents and driving discord. And maybe saved your own life.

2. Drive for the car directly in front of you.

This technique is well worth mastering. Over 90% of the cars on the road are designed in such a way that, when you drive behind them, you can still see through their front windshields. (Exceptions are any type of truck, most vans and 4-wheel drives.) Get in the habit of looking *through* the windshield of the car in front of you and trying to anticipate how the driver of that car will react to things. Once you master this technique, you will find that you are reacting smoothly and professionally to things that might otherwise have taken you by surprise. In fact, this technique is so addictive that, if you should find yourself behind a vehicle that doesn't permit this kind of view, you will feel compelled to pass it, if only to find a car that you can follow and look through at the same time!

3. Play Pacman, mentally, with your own car. Know what is around you at all times.

Most drivers know that the mirrors in the car can be used to fill the blind spots around them. Fewer realize that regular "sweeps" of these mirrors allow you to create a *continuous mental picture* of what is around you at all times. Then, when you check your mirror, you will not find a new situation every time you look; you will merely update your existing mental picture. Again, this habit might take a while to develop but is worthwhile. Say, for example, on your last check, your rear-view mirror indicated a car just behind and to the right of your vehicle, but your next sweep shows the vehicle is not there. You would realize right away that the vehicle in question is now most likely in your right-rear blind spot, and act accordingly. On the other hand, if you "recreate" your position with each new check you would simply see an empty slot behind you and assume you have the road to yourself.

4. When watching a vehicle that looks like it might pull into your lane from a parked position, watch the front wheel, rather than the whole car.

It's a matter of physics and geometry. It is entirely possible that the driver of the other vehicle doesn't see you and will drive directly into your lane. If you watch the whole vehicle, you might not perceive its movement soon enough. Even the slightest movement of the vehicle could be enough for it to reach your lane, so, by the time you conclude (or perceive) that the vehicle is actually moving, it might be too late. On the other hand, the front wheel turns many times for each incremental movement of the chassis, so by watching *it*, you will instantly be able to tell if the fool really is going to drive smack-dab into your lane.

5. Turn off the radio occasionally and *listen* to your car.

Many mechanical problems, especially safety-related ones, announce themselves well in advance to the driver who bothers to listen. Listen to your vehicle both at rest (at a stop light) and at speed, to determine whether any new sounds may have cropped up. If so, get them checked out pronto. (Ticking or tapping means a valve problem; roaring usually means a potential exhaust problem; metallic slaps indicate internal engine problems; grinding noises when driving point to a water pump problem, and when stopping, to a brake problem.)

SHIFT FOR YOURSELF

You can tell a true car person by their shifters. The ones who take driving seriously use a manual. Sure I've heard all that stuff about, "The automatic is better for stop-and-go driving"; "I need it for my spouse"; and even — my favourite — "The torque curve of the engine is better matched to the gear ratios of the automatic." Bull-do. Automatics are a compromise, they add weight to the car, they decrease fuel economy, they cost a lot to repair and they never seem to shift when they should. With a manual, the driver is in full control of the car. The driver can choose whether to shift for power (flooring the throttle and staying in each gear until the torque kicks in) or economy (going easy on the throttle and getting into the high gears a.s.a.p.). The driver can also choose when to shift down in a hurry, either to brake (shift down, no gas) or to speed up (shift down and hit the gas). The driver can even do second gear starts on ice if need be. And, in an absolute emergency — in spite of the theoretical damage risk to the catalytic converter — the driver can perform a push start using just a little elbow grease and a little gravity. Automatics do none of this.

In fairness to the teckies out there, it is true that, with turbo-charged cars, the power band of the turbo engine will mesh more seamlessly with an automatic than a manual. But, before you get carried away, keep in mind that when you match a turbo to an automatic, it is almost impossible to drive without activating the turbo. Therefore, the turbo is on forever. Therefore, gas economy suffers. With a turbo mated to a manual shifter, you can control the turbo simply by keeping a light touch on the gas. I repeat: I like the manual gearbox.

6. Buy the loudest horn and brightest lights your car can handle.

Many cars come from the factory with horns that sound like rabid ducks. Although it may be true that professional truckers use their horns and lights to hold little dialogues with each other in some peculiar kind of code, the average driver uses brights and the horn sparingly, and usually only in emergencies. With this in mind, you owe it to yourself to make sure your messages, when sent, are received.

7. Make your lights work for you, not against you.

Again, most cars come with lights that meet the minimum federal standards...period. For about $100 you can upgrade your lights to state-of-the-art quartz halogen and your horn to something that would not seem inappropriate even on the Day of Judgement. When you have proper lights, and you want to signal someone, they'll get the message real fast. (Note: Headlamps with this newer technology can no longer be installed by the owner. Special equipment is needed to align them. This is not an expensive procedure, and, given the alternative, is well worth the money.)

8. Try to recall what you *really* learned in Driver's Ed. If you are not sure, take a refresher course.

A lot of the things we do when we drive we believe to be correct. But they're not. Through a process psychologists call "convenient memory," human beings have an amazing ability to relearn things the way they want and to convince themselves that's the way those things always were. One example, of many, is the way most drivers pull into the left lane when they want to pass. In Driver's Ed., most of us were taught, "Signal, then check your mirror to make sure the lane is free and will be free for the amount of time it takes you to make your manoeuvre, then proceed." In real life, most of us have now substituted the following mental sequence: "Signal, then check your mirror to make sure the lane is sufficiently open for you to make the lane change regardless of whether any other rapidly approaching vehicle already in that lane is about to fill the space." More on this below.

THE LANGUAGE OF HORNS

Did you ever notice that there is a "language" to honking? There is. Maybe nobody in Driver's Ed. ever brought it to your attention, but there is really a whole system of etiquette involving the use of your horn. Let's look at an example. You are at a stop light and the car in front of you — the car closest to the intersection — doesn't notice when the light turns green. What to do? Honk, of course. How? Two or three very short taps will do the trick. In horn talk, two or three very short taps means, "Oops I know you are really a pretty good driver. You're just having a bad day and I wanted to remind you about the green light." It works every time.

If you think I'm making this up, try sending a different message in the same situation. Instead of two or three light taps when the car ahead of you fails to move, lean on that horn button and let a blast out. Did the car in front of you move? Not likely. More likely, the driver is still in the same spot only this time he or she is looking in the rear-view mirror and insulting your mother. If, moreover, the driver in front is a 150-kilogram professional wrestler, then by now he's reached your front fender and he's attempting to do body work on your vehicle. Without any special tools, that is. The point here is that a loud prolonged honk means, "Listen you moron, I've got better things to do than wait for you to figure out which pedal makes the car go forward." A loud prolonged honk should only be used in cases of extreme emergency, such as when another car doesn't know you're there and is about to hit you.

Finally, a special note to all you owners of small economy cars. Some genius in the engineering department has

> determined that a small little car should have a small little horn. As a result, when an emergency does come up and you need to lean on your horn, you may find that not much happens. A yelp or a squeal perhaps. But not a true honk. The solution? For under $30 you can replace the horn on your present car with one that sounds more macho. It's a ten-minute job that any garage can do. And a pretty good investment in safety, besides.

9. Expect the worst.

Of all the rules I've given, this is possibly the most important. It is so essential to Car Kung Fu driving skills that it should never be trivialized or minimized. Simply put, this principle says, "Assume the drivers on the road with you will do the stupidest thing possible when you get near them."

Imagine that you are on a two-lane highway in the left lane cruising at the legal maximum, or perhaps just slightly faster. Looking up the highway you see that you are about to pass two cars moving along in the right lane. Because you are a Car Kung Fu driver, you don't let it go at that. You examine those two cars closely as you approach them. You realize that, although both are definitely going slower than you, the lead car in the right lane is also going more slowly than the car just behind it. You reach the conclusion that the car behind will likely wish to pass what it considers to be the slower vehicle (the same way you consider both vehicles to be slow relative to your own car). The most logical assumption is that the driver of the tail car (the faster of the two in that lane) will check his mirrors, see you about to pass in the left lane, wait for you to pass, and then make his own lane-change and pass manoeuvres. Nothing could be further from the truth! Most often — and I have tested this on dozens of highways all over the world — the tail driver will glance in his mirror, notice your car coming up fast, assume that, simply by signalling, he has the absolute right to move into the left lane and cut you off, and then proceed to do just that. This will, of course, result in your own car almost tail-gating his car, since you were going faster than the two other cars to start with. And you will have to wait until that other driver, now blocking you off in the left lane, completes his passing manoeuvre at a speed which will seem excruciatingly slow to you, but probably blood-curdling to him. All in all, the likelihood of an accident or a miscalculation will have increased dramatically. So, in a nutshell: expect the worst, not the best, from other drivers. And you'll often get it.

10. Watch out for trucks.

I remember a young lady who came up to see me after a course and told me how she had recently lost her car — and, at the same time, almost lost her life. "I was making a right turn as I always do," she explained, "and halfway through my turn I noticed that the large truck which had been on my left wasn't going straight, it was turning right with me. And, because of its size, and the narrow corner, its middle part was coming right for my car as it made its turn. I honked like crazy but by the time the driver reacted, my car was crushed."

In North America over 50% of all commercial goods are moved by trucks. That puts an awful lot of big rigs on the road. Most truckers are pretty good drivers, and pretty careful too. But, with all those trucks on the road, all it takes is a few bad apples to cause trouble. And make no mistake: get into a tug-of-war with a truck and you lose. No contest.

What's the Car Kung Fu secret to avoiding arguments with trucks? Simple: avoid trucks. If you have to share space with them, stay to the front or rear of the larger vehicle. Under no circumstances should you ever flank a truck for any distance; i.e., don't stay somewhere around the middle part of the truck's cab. Most trucks are blind there. Their mirrors just don't give the driver a clear picture. Drivers who flank trucks on long highway drives — perhaps trying to confuse police radar — are taking risks they may not fully appreciate. Stay away!

FINDING THE ESCAPE ROUTE

One of the most important principles in defensive driving is imagining, while you drive, where you might throw your car in an emergency. This most precious technique takes a lot for granted. It assumes the driver has enough mental processing room left to keep track of this at all times. It assumes the driver is aware that, statistically, it is always an easier and safer manoeuvre to steer a moving car out of danger than it is to apply the brakes and hope the car will stop before it hits whatever obstacle has come up. I forced myself to learn this habit decades ago and I believe it has saved my life at least twice.

Let me tell you of one instance. Late on a Saturday night, on a two-lane urban roadway, I came up behind a slow-moving car in the left lane weaving a little from side to side. I decided that my best move was to pass it on the right — something that normally I would reserve only for emergencies. So I did. Just as I was passing, I was shocked to see that the driver, for reasons I will never understand, decided to turn into the right lane. My lane. He steered his car directly into the side of my car. My options were few. Honking might have worked, but I suspected the other driver was drunk and I didn't want to gamble on his reaction time. Braking would not have worked — a collision would have resulted for sure. In the fraction of a second I had to make up my mind, I yanked the steering wheel to the right and drove up onto the sidewalk. A collision was avoided. The only reason I could do what I did was that, out of years of habit, I had already determined that the sidewalk was empty of pedestrians before I made my manoeuvre. My mental picture of the escape route was pre-programmed and cleared. Always leave yourself an "out."

MEET JOHNNY SPEED

Here I'm going to do something that, as far as I know, has never been done before. I am going to reveal the secret rules of the "crazies," the speeders who zip by you as if they don't have a care in the world. By doing interviews over the years with people who lust for speed, I have come to realize that these drivers are not moving randomly. There are unwritten rules to the way they drive. While these drivers are most dangerous to others driving in the same style, they can and do cause problems for innocents who stumble into their paths unintentionally. Here is an extract of an interview I did with a driver who admitted that he always speeds, always passes everyone and always gets where he is going ahead of everyone else.

Note: The subject of this interview is a gentleman, 29 years of age, who has been driving since the age of 17. His driving record is above average and, at the time of the interview, he had a 5-star (top) rating with his insurer. While he was willing to share his secrets with me — on the condition that he remain anonymous — he was unwilling to see anything wrong with the way he drove. He made the point over and over that he is probably a safer driver than many others because he pays such great attention to the road. The only time he becomes dangerous, he admitted, is when he is "challenged." It is my personal belief that there are tens of thousands like this fellow driving on North American roads today. I think the normal driver would do well to learn what makes this guy tick — and how to avoid him at all costs.

I move along in the left lane just slightly faster than the traffic flow. I don't know what the speed limit is and, frankly, I don't care. You see, I am not a speeder. I am a mover. There is a difference. The important thing is to be going just slightly faster than everyone else. That's the key, you see. That entitles me to use that left lane, legally. And it is important that I always get where I am going early, that I am always at the stop light first, that I always get to my destination first. It is silly to say that I believe that anyone else in the city is going the exact same route that I am, from A to B, but I convince myself that, if anybody was, then I would be the first to arrive. Do you get it?

People who hog that left lane make me nuts. They have no right to it, don't you see? I need that left lane to keep my speed up. I need it desperately. I do not believe I am dangerous since, as I said, I am only going slightly faster than everyone else. But when someone blocks me off in that left lane, that's when I suppose I could become a little dangerous. I feel trapped. I know that my time on this run will be poor and it's not my fault. I take it very personally. When this happens I will first blink my lights or honk. And even by now I'm already a little mad, because I'm right on the back bumper of the car that's blocking me, and if the driver were half as good as he probably thinks he is, he would have noticed me by now and moved out of my way.

By this time, I admit, I am really nervous. The adrenalin is pumping. If the driver in front of me pulls over to the right lane to let me pass, I will wave in the mirror to thank him. But often the opposite will happen. The person will tense up over the wheel and pretend to ignore me. This makes my blood boil. Left-lane hogs, especially the righteous ones, are fanatics and they are more dangerous than anyone else, as far as I am concerned. If I think I am being deliberately blocked, I will use every trick I know to pass the car in front of me, including passing on the right, passing over a double line, and once I even went over a concrete median. It becomes very personal. And it happens more often that you would believe.

Another thing is that every now and then, maybe once every two or three days, I will come across someone driving the same way as I am. It's easy for us to spot each other since we are both trying to move slightly faster than everyone else. Pretty soon we realize that we are the only two cars on the road that are still there. What happens next is anyone's guess. Sometimes, if it's a long drive or an open highway, one car will play leader and the other will follow at a pretty constant distance. Then, after a few kilometres, we will switch positions. It's a way of saving face, of saying, "Hey, neither one of us is any better than the other." You have to realize that this takes place without any communication. No mobile phones, no lights, no honks. We just know what to do. It's like we have driver ESP.

Sometimes things get nasty. If I meet someone driving like me and we are both in a rush, it becomes an out-and-out race. Pretty soon the rest of the traffic is unimportant and we are racing each other, dodging in and out of other cars like they were standing still. Even at this point, it need not be dangerous, as long as certain rules are followed, as long as respect is shown.

I can't explain exactly the point at which one driver in this situation would show that he has no respect for the other driver, but, believe me, I'd know it in a second on the road. If this happens, if disrespect is shown, there are no longer any rules. I have never been in an accident but I know the closest I've come to one is when I started to race a strange car and it became "personal."

So what's the lesson to be learned from this extremely dangerous individual (although he himself might not know just how dangerous he is)?

Drive to survive! Leave your Charles Bronson vigilante hat at home, follow the Car Kung Fu rules of the road, stay out of the left lane unless you mean to use it, and don't mess with people you don't know who are willing to do any-thing —literally — to make a point!

WHAT ABOUT DRIVING FOR BETTER FUEL ECONOMY?

Recently I loaned my '78 Mazda GLC to a friend. You have to realize, to appreciate this story, that I love this car. Not because it is great looking; it isn't. Not because it is state of the art; it isn't. I love it because it is reliable and it gets over 35 km to the gallon even in city driving. Now, here's a mystery. My friend drives the car for a few days and then complains about the terrible fuel consumption. Terrible consumption?

I look the car over mechanically and it looks fine. What's going on? Suddenly, enlightenment. I ask my friend to take the car to the corner store so I can see how he drives. Sure enough, I notice that his driving habits are very different from mine. The Mazda has a 4-speed manual transmission. When I drive, I spend as little time as possible in first and second gear. I get to third gear almost immediately, and then, as soon as I can, I shift to fourth. This method of driving takes more time but, as far as I know, saves engine wear and also saves gasoline.

My friend has a different style. He spends a long time in first gear, building speed. Then he stays in second for as long as he can. When the engine screams in pain, he shifts to third. In city traffic he almost never hits fourth gear. The bottom line? I calculate his consumption is almost 35% more than mine. With the cost of gasoline what it is, 35% can make a big difference to a fuel bill.

My friend and I are probably at different ends of the spectrum. I spend too much time shifting, and he spends too little. Most of you are somewhere in the middle. It is worth taking a few minutes to consider exactly how economical your driving style is. For maximum economy, you should shift into the higher gears earlier, not later. If you discover that you have to slow down, fine, shift temporarily to a lower gear. Under normal circumstances you should not hear your engine revving at all. If you hear your engine revving loudly just before you change gears, you are waiting too long. And, chances are, your gas bills are higher than they should be.

11

Questions And Answers

After two decades of Car Kung Fu seminars, I have noticed that people ask the same questions over and over. Here are those I have been asked most often, along with the appropriate answers.

Q: Like many so-called objective car magazines, Car Kung Fu seems to favour Japanese cars. Why?

A: Why, indeed? In 1990 — a time when the domestics could hardly say that the Japanese invasion was still taking them by surprise — a major consumer survey concluded that 82% of Japanese-car owners were satisfied with their cars, compared with 67% of the domestic owners. In terms of dealer service, 61% of the Japanese-car owners were happy, compared with 44% of the domestic owners. Frankly, I am tired of arguing about this. The numbers speak louder than words. Detroit has had 20 years to get its act together, and it hasn't. What Detroit companies have done, however, is use their capital base to buy into the Japanese companies. If you can't beat 'em, join 'em? I am an optimist. Detroit will eventually figure out what it is doing wrong. I just don't think it will be in my lifetime.

Q: How do I store my car? Do I really need nitrogen for the tires and aviation fuel for the gas tank?

A: A heated garage is preferable to an unheated garage, and both are better than outside exposure. Some of you will recall hearing that heated garages can encourage rusting. This is true only if you drive the car in and out of the heated garage throughout the winter. If the car is left alone, a heated garage is fine. And if you have no garage and the car is left exposed, get a car cover. The car cover will cost a few hundred dollars but will protect the body from some of the ravages of an extreme climate. It will not, however, protect the inner panels from the condensation or dew cycle which takes place every 24 hours.

Now what about all those little tips and tricks you've been told are essential to car storage? Things like putting the car on blocks; filling the tires with nitrogen gas; running aviation fuel through the fuel lines; pouring motor oil in the spark holes; draining the gas tank; draining the rad; and all that other neat stuff. Here's the scoop: You can do all that if you want to, but all you really need to do is disconnect the battery from the car and connect a timed low-amp charger to it. Setting the charger for about ten minutes a day is all it takes. When you want to start the car, follow these steps. Reconnect the battery. Disconnect temporarily the ignition circuit and then crank the car for 15 seconds to build oil pressure. Reconnect the ignition wires and start the car. Just how reliable is this bare-bones method? Very reliable. I used it recently to fire up my showcar, a '68 Mercury Cougar, after the car had been left idle for two solid years. The car started right away.

Q: Do I need to buy extra insurance coverage when renting?

A: As you know, the price quoted by the rental agencies for renting a car does not generally include insurance. If you damage the rental car, or another car, you pay. Many consumers, unhappy with this arrangement, agree to purchase extra coverage from the rental agency when signing the rental agreement. Trouble is, in most cases this extra coverage costs as much as, or more than, the cost of renting the car! Smell a rip off here? Absolutely. It took a few years for the consumer watchdogs in the US and Canada to complete their investigations, but it now seems conclusive that this extra coverage is needlessly overpriced and actually a source of hidden profits to the renter. What to do? Try using a credit card, such as American Express, which includes coverage automatically, at no charge, any time you use the card. Overall, this is likely your best bet. You can also arrange with your own insurance company to sell you either one-time or full-time rental coverage for an additional premium on your base policy.

Q: I have a lemon. What do I do?

A: It now seems there are as many different laws on the
      books to help consumers as there are different types of
      cars! My own research shows that consumers who rely
      on particular laws such as "Lemon Laws" or "Arbitra-
      tion Laws" don't get the results they want in the time
      they wanted to get them. Myself, I like the old fash-
      ioned route: Small Claims Court. Every city, province,
      or state has them. You don't need a lawyer. The cost
      varies from place to place but generally should be no
      more than $50 — and usually a lot less. Time also
      varies. Just getting your case scheduled before the
      judge could take anywhere from a week to a year.
      Once again it depends. The trial itself will, I promise
      you, be quite speedy. You might think that your prob-
      lem is something only Perry Mason could do justice
      to. In fact, the judge will likely ask both sides some
      pointed questions and then solve the whole thing in
      under ten minutes. The odds, by the way, are heavily
      in favour of the little guy in this court.
          Does winning mean you get paid? Yes and no. Yes,
      in that once you have a legal judgement that can be
      executed, you can always have a bailiff seize property
      from the other side if you are not paid off. On the
      other hand, there are people and companies who have
      practically made a science of skipping out on legal
      debts. They might even move or declare bankruptcy to
      beat you. Practically, however, the total amount
      awarded by a Small Claims Court is unlikely to be so
      onerous that the defendant contemplates bankruptcy or
      other evasive action. And, if the people you are suing
      are still in active business, they will likely prefer to
      pay you off quickly, rather than damage their commer-
      cial reputation further. One last reminder: Most small

claims disputes are settled out of court, between the time the claim is filed and the time scheduled for trial. If you want to increase your chances of getting a quick settlement, you must file your claim to start the process. If you don't play, you can't win.

Q: How do I get a confiscated car?

A: Easy: park your own car in a tow zone!
Just kidding. In fact, I get asked this question a lot. Nowadays there seems to be more money in writing about confiscated cars than in actually buying them, though. Here are the Car Kung Fu basics on confiscated or surplus cars.
Yes, these things really do exist. The seller in virtually all confiscated or surplus cases is usually the government, through one of its many agencies, or, occasionally, a trustee for bankruptcy on behalf of the creditors of the bankrupt party.
The deals are not particularly special, being, on average, only slightly better than what you would get if you were a licensed automotive wholesaler attending the regular auctions. Of course, keep in mind that regular wholesalers do, in fact, shop for these same government "bargains," and the presence of professionals at these government sales keeps prices in line and reasonable.
Tracking down the various sales in your area is easy. First, you simply watch the daily papers every day under "Legal Notices." If you are really keen, you may contact the local branches of the various government agencies and request that you be put on the mailing lists. (There is sometimes a fee for this service.)

Tracking down bargains outside of your area is a pain, however. Unless you want to do this as a career, forget about travelling outside of your area to look for bargains.

Here are some agencies to contact.

In Canada:

- Crown Assets Disposal, Ottawa.

In the US:

- General Services Administration, Washington, DC;
- US Department of Defense, Washington, DC;
- US Customs Service, Washington, DC;
- Internal Revenue, Washington, DC.

Also contact local police departments, local bankruptcy trustees, and local insurance companies.

For what it's worth, in all the years I've been working with cars, I've had only one student who ever connected in this way. The gentleman earned his living as an insurance agent and, when one of his clients got into financial trouble, he immediately contacted the branch of the bank that he knew held security on the client's vehicle. He then bid on the vehicle — against other bidders — and ended up paying about $5,500 for a 3-year old domestic sedan that might have cost him $6,500 to $7,000 under normal conditions. A good deal, yes. But a steal? You tell me!

Q: What about "collectible" cars?

A: The way collectible cars are advertised, you'd think you can have your cake and eat it too. Drive a car that you get a kick out of and one that also appreciates, just like an investment! The bad news? Anyone who tells you that you can run these cars like you would a regular car is funning you. The more kilometres on the clock, the less likely you are to see your money back. My own '68 Cougar GT is a collectible, sure. But with only 10,000 original km on the thing, I can't pretend I take it out that often. Before you start playing the collectable game, get advice from a pro, an appraiser who can tell you what you're really buying. (Your insurance company should help you find one. If not, change insurance companies!) Buy a collectible with your head, not your heart!

Q: I've heard of a car "hotline" that bills me automatically for the latest price info. How does it work?

A: And you'll be hearing of these a lot more, I promise. The recent "900" call technology allows experts to answer your questions, with the charges automatically billed to your own home. One of the oldest, and most highly recommended of these services is Car-puter, at 1-900-226-CARS. The service features up-to-date pricing on new and used vehicles. (US only.)

Q: What is the "three-minute tire fix" I've heard people refer to?

A: This is a case in which the story behind the story is more interesting than the story itself. The three-minute tire fix refers to the inflator-in-a-can products that came on to the market during the late seventies. The products themselves are excellent. All brands are more

or less the same. They really can inflate a seriously
messed-up tire in under three minutes, and get you
safely to the nearest garage. I carry a can in each of
my cars. And my students are advised to do so as well.

More interesting, however, is that these products are
a classic example of delayed marketing. Often, when a
really good product comes to market, the manufacturer
may not have the confidence, or the money, to really
let the consumer know the product has arrived. By the
time the news campaigns start, years may have gone
by, and the product is no longer new. This happened
with the tire inflators, and it also happened with
WD-40, a really neat lubricant and moisture-displacer
which was on the market almost ten years before the
maker started to promote it. I also carry WD-40 in all
my cars. The chemical has this weird ability to drive
moisture from ignition parts and get you started when
all else fails!

Q: How you drive "practically for free"?

A: This is a reference to my car ownership strategy based
     on buying used cars only. (See my book *The Used Car
     Believer's System,* Doubleday, 1982.) The point is
     that, regardless of the year or the inflation rate, the
     market value of a working used car seldom drops
     below about $1,800. This means that, to look at the
     matter from the other side, if you have $1,800 to
     spend, you can buy a 6-year-old economy car, or a 15-
     year-old luxury car, or even a 30-year-old sports car.
     No matter what the car or the year, working machinery
     will always get this amount on the open market. To
     make this odd fact work for you, spend about $3,000
     for the most recent car you can get your hands on,

keep the car a minimum of 6 years (easy if you follow
Car Kung Fu) and then sell the car for no less than
$1,800. This means that your depreciation, not count-
ing repairs, is $1,200 for 6 years, or about $200 a year.
That's practically free, in my book.

Q: Any special advice for when you are stopped by
police, or involved in an accident?

A: Yes: say nothing. Statements made at this time are
legally admissable later on. When caught speeding,
the driver will first try to "confess" his or her way out
of it with the police officer: "Yes, I was slightly over
the limit but I have a clean record, I meant well, my
wife is pregnant, and I have only three days to live...."
The police officer smiles and writes the ticket anyway.
When the court case comes up, the defendant suddenly
denies speeding at all. The officer then refers to the
notes of the conversation and...game over. The same
applies to an accident. If you admit anything at the
time of the accident you may technically be in viola-
tion of your arrangement with your insurer. Contrac-
tually, you are supposed to stonewall.

Q: Can you talk your way out of a ticket?

A: Personally? Not a chance. If anything, something in
my demeanour makes the arresting officer seem to
want to upgrade my speeding tickets to something
more intellectually stimulating — like First Degree
Murder. I have, however, seen a number of my students successfully talk themselves out of a ticket. One
was a salesman so slick he could have made a go at
selling bibles in Baghdad. He convinced the officer

that he was speeding to catch up with another driver to whom he had given wrong directions, and he was worried that if he didn't catch her, she would end up lost. And the best sweet-talker I've ever seen was a 75-year-old man who was, generally, tougher, hardier and shrewder than many professional wrestlers. However, the moment the officer pulled him over, an astounding aging process took place. Suddenly he was a weak, frail and almost blind old man. He called the officer "son" a lot. The police officer was in such a hurry to get away from that sickly old man he almost left a trail of rubber behind him.

Q: I want to help the environment. What can I do?

A: An environmentally friendly car is like a rubber bullet — a triumph of theory over utility. Still, if you insist on going the distance, avoid leaded gas, have your exhaust gases analyzed on a regular basis, and make sure your mechanic recycles your oil, and antifreeze. If your air conditioner needs service, make sure that nothing is released into the air during the process. All these services are now available, but not all mechanics offer them.

Q: What is the Car Kung Fu "buyer's club" technique?

A: Many people have buying power which they underutilize or fail to utilize at all. To take one example, the first time I moved into a condominium complex, I immediately went around to all the local merchants — garages included — and told them that, if they offered everyone in the condo 10% off everything they sold, they would get a free mention in each edition of the condo newsletter. The merchants loved the idea — it was better for them than "take-a-chance" advertising — and so did the condo newsletter. Everyone who used the plan got top service and great prices. As far as I know, the plan is still in force. You can do the same with any local shop in your area. Are you part of a condo, a bowling team, an enthusiasts' club? Can you assemble four or five others who would be willing to patronize the same mechanic in return for good service and a discount? Think about it. The best Car Kung Fu techniques are also the simplest. This one works every time.

Q: What do *you* carry in your car? And how?

A: Buy a laundry basket from any hardware shop. The new plastic ones are best. Into the basket put:

- an all-in-one socket set;
- a screwdriver set;
- a crescent wrench;
- battery cables;
- a flashlight;
- baking soda (for fires);
- a camera (for accidents, as evidence of what "really" happened);
- tire inflator in a can;
- gloves, hat, umbrella;
- a roll of quarters;
- a map of your city;
- a trunk tie-down cord and scissors;
- an extra fan belt to fit your car;
- a can of WD-40 (dries out wet ignitions);
- a can of mixed nuts (smoked almonds, if possible).

Put the basket in your trunk. That's it. Twenty years of car journalism says you have a kit which will see you through almost any emergency that can come up!

Q: How can I get better gas consumption?

A: Drive slower! Or, at the very least, *smoother*. You can take it as gospel that the car companies are doing everything they can to keep consumption figures down these days — they have to. It's the law! Aside from that, there is little left to be done. Most gas-saving doodads don't work. However, a major study done by a US oil company showed that the average driver can get up to 30% better fuel economy by driving slower, and staying in the upper gear ranges longer. Think about it!

Q: Is it true that you can cool down an overheating car by turning the heater on?

A: Theoretically, yes. The heat pouring into your car is coming from the engine and that means there is less heat in the engine to cause problems. Use this technique in an emergency only, though.

Q: I have heard of "idiot lights" but what are "idiot circuits"?

A: On many new cars there is a circuit that monitors how close you get to the red line on the tachometer — i.e., how many revs you do in each gear. In the old days, if you wanted to, you could over-rev the car and risk blowing the headgasket of the engine. Now you can't — the engine cuts out automatically. What happens if there is a life-or-death emergency and you really need every ounce of power the engine can deliver? A lawsuit, probably.

Q: What is your dumbest "Car Kung Fu" tip?

A: In an emergency, you can wash your hands by turning on the windshield spritzers and sticking your hand in front of the nozzle. Hey — don't laugh until you've tried it!

Reference List

American Automobile
Association
1000 AAA Dr.
Heathrow, FL 32746-5063
(407)444-8000

Automobile Importers of
America
1725 Jefferson Davis Hwy.
Suite 1002
Arlington, VA 22202
(703)979-5550

Automotive Industries
Association of Canada
1272 Wellington St.
Ottawa, Ontario
K1Y 3A7
Canada
(613)728-5821

Automotive Information
Council
29200 Southfield Rd.
Suite 111
Southfield, MI 48076
(313)559-5922

Automotive Market
Research Council
300 Sylvan Ave.
Box 1638
Englewood Cliffs, NJ 07632
(201)481-3118

Automotive President's
Council
300 Sylvan Ave.
Box 1638
Englewood Cliffs, NJ 07632
(201)569-8500

Automotive Safety
Foundation
1776 Massachusetts Ave. NW
Washington, DC 20036
(202)569-8500

Automotive Service
Association
1901 Airport Fwy.
Suite 100
Bedford, TX 76021-0929
(817)283-6205

**British Automobile
Manufacturers Association**
1 Sound Shore Dr.
Greenwich, CT 06830
(203)622-1723

Car Care Council
One Grand Lake Dr.
Port Clinton, OH 43452
(419)734-5343

Center For Auto Safety
2001 S Street SW
Washington, DC 20008
(202)328-7700

Automotive Programs
1515 Wilson Blvd.
Suite 600
Arlington, VA 22209
(703)276-0100

**Environmental Protection
Agency**
401 M St. SW
Washington, DC 20460
(202)382-4700

Federal Trade Commission
Pennsylvania Ave. at
6th St., NW
Washington, DC 20580
(202)326-2177

**Insurance Institute for
Highway Safety**
1005 North Glebe Rd.
Suite 800
Arlington, VA 22001
(703)247-1500

**Interstate Commerce
Commission**
ICC Building
12th and Constitution Ave.
Washington, DC 20423
(202)275-7348

**Japan Automobile
Manufacturers
Association, Inc.**
1050 17th St. NW
Suite 410
Washington, DC 20036
(202)296-8537

**Motor Vehicle
Manufacturers Association
of the US, Inc.
(MVMA)**
7430 Second Ave.
Suite 300
Detroit, MI 48202
(313)872-4311

**National Automobile
Dealers Association (NADA)**
8400 Westpark Dr.
McLean, VA 22102
(703)821-7000

**National Highway Traffic
Safety Administration**
ICC Building
12th and Constitution Ave.
Washington, DC 20423
(202)366-1836

**US Department of
Transportation**
400 Seventh St. SW
Washington, DC 20590
(202)366-1111

Major Manufacturers

Note that some numbers may not be accessible from all provinces and all states.

Acura   (800)382-2238
Alfa Romeo   (201)871-1234
Aston Martin   (203)359-2259
Audi (800)822-2834
Avanti (800)548-6350
Bentley (800)777-6923
BMW (201)307-4263
Buick (800)521-7300
Cadillac (800)458-8006
Chevrolet (800)222-1020
Chrysler (800)992-1997
Daihatsu (800)777-7070
Dodge (800)992-1997
Eagle (800)992-1997
Ferrari (201)393-4058
Ford (800)521-4140
Geo (800)222-1020
Honda   See Your Owner's
        Manual
Hyundai   (714)890-6000
Infiniti (800)522-0990
Isuzu (800)255-3987
Jaguar (201)592-5200
Lexus (800)255-3987

Lincoln/Mercury
        (800)521-4140
Lotus (404)822-4566
Maserati (301)646-6400
Mazda (714)727-1990
Mercedes (800)222-0100
Mitsubishi (800)222-0037
Nissan (800)647-7261
Oldsmobile (517)377-5000
Peugeot (800)345-5549
Plymouth (800)992-1997
Pontiac (800)762-2737
Porsche (800)272-7677
Range Rover (301)731-9040
Rolls-Royce (800)777-6923
Saab (203)795-5671
Sterling (305)477-7400
Subaru (609)488-3278
Suzuki (800)877-6900
Toyota (800)331-4331
Volkswagen
        (800)444-VWUS
Volvo (800)767-4740
Yugo (201)825-4600

Index

About The Author

Robert Appel is the star of "Cartalk," the longest-running syndicated show on CBC radio. He has appeared on AM-Buffalo, "Lifetime," Global's News at Noon, and "Good Morning America" to talk about car ownership and the automobile industry. In 1971 Appel began teaching a series of seminars at McGill University on a "total defensive strategy" for car owners. He eventually came up with another name for the course: "Car Kung Fu."

Appel's published works include:

Used Car Handbook (Van Nostrand, 1978)

Rebound System (Harper & Row, 1982)

Used Car Believer's System (Doubleday, 1982)

Car Owner's Survivor Guide (Ballantine, 1986).

The GST Handbook (Self-Counsel, 1990)

Appel currently lives near Toronto, Canada.